Diet recommendations for arteriosclerosis and infarction

Please check these recommendations always with a nutrition consultant, therapist, doctor or dietician. The recipes and the list of ingredients are supporting the conventional medical therapy.
The calorie disclosures of fresh ingredients (fruit and vegetables) vary according to quality and time of harvest. The contents were checked by a dietician and a nutrition consultant for the Traditional Chinese Medicine (TCM).

Author:
©2017 Josef Miligui
www.ebns.at

AF285342

Source:
The lists are created from the EBNS database for nutritional counseling. The database is used by dietitians, therapists and doctors for advising the patient / client.

Literature:
The specialist literature and the training documents of the German and Austrian dietary and traditional Chinese medicine serve as a knowledge base. We have used the documents as a basis of knowledge, adapted it to our experience and completed them.
http://di-book.com

Title Photo:
©2008 Erika Weixlbaumer

Production and publishing:
BoD – Books on Demand, Norderstedt
ISBN: 9783752861549

Diet recommendations for DIETETICS - Metabolism - Heart and circulation - Arteriosclerosis (arterial calcification) and infarction

1   Treatment strategy

Bring blood fat values and blood pressure into the normal range.
Treat hypertension.
Reach normal weight.
Use high-quality fat (rapeseed oil, olive oil, linseed oil, walnut oil).
Use high-quality foods (omega-3 fatty acids, coenzyme Q10, vitamins B and vitamin C, fresh herbs).
Exercise and relaxation

2 Avoid

Overweight.
Animal fat.

3 Breakfast

4 Snack

5 Lunch

6   Afternoon

7   Dinner

8   Any time

9 Recipes

(recommendable) = You can use more.
(little) = You should use less than specified or omit.

9.1 Andalusian fish pot

Strengthens immune system, prevents cancer, dissolves stagnation, promotes weight loss. Good to fight immunodeficiency, loss of appetite, flatulence, high blood pressure, depressions, diabetes, diarrhea, stimulates appetite.
Cooking time approx. 30 min
Calories p. portion: 348
4 portions
Allergens: ADLO

Quantity of ingredients:
Basic recipe for a vegetable soup (nutritious) 2 cups / 500g. (recommended)
Onion (spring onion) 2 pieces / 40g. (yes)
Olive oil 1 table spoon / 20g. (recommended)
Lemon peel 1/2 piece / 3g. (yes)
Bay leaf 1 piece / 1g. (recommended)
Potato 5/8 oz / 200g. (recommended)
Cod 3/4 lbs / 300g. (yes)
White wine 4 table spoons / 80g. (yes)
Lemon juice 1/2 teaspoon / 10g. (yes)
Salt 1 pinch / 1g. (little)
Pepper (ground) 1 pinch / 0,2g. (yes)
Parsley 1 table spoon / 15g. (recommended)
White bread (wheat bread) 8 slices / 250g. (little)

Cooking instructions:
Boil the vegetable broth with small spring onion, olive oil, grated lemon peel and bay leaf. Boil covered for 10 minutes. Add the peeled, diced potatoes and boil in about 8 minutes. Add fish pieces and white wine and switch to small heat. In the slightly boiling broth put the fish and boil it a few minutes. Season with lemon juice, salt and pepper. Serve with parsley sprinkled.
White bread as a side dish.

9.2   Antipasti

Improves blood circulation, anti-inflammatory, relieves pain. Diuretic, promotes digestion, reduces blood pressure. antioxidativ, antibacterial, affects anorexia, improves digestion, flatulence, stomach weakness, stimulating.
Cooking time approx. 40 min
Calories p. portion: 100
3 portions
Allergens:

Quantity of ingredients:
Pepperoni 1 piece / 5g. (yes)
Lemon juice 1 table spoon / 10g. (yes)
Aubergine 1 piece / 300g. (recommended)
Tomato 4 pieces / 200g. (recommended)
Zucchini 5/8 oz / 200g. (recommended)
Lemon peel 1/2 piece / 3g. (yes)
Olive oil 1 table spoon / 15g. (recommended)
Basil (fresh) 8 leaves / 5g. (recommended)
Salt 1 pinch / 0,5g. (little)
Coriander 1/2 teaspoon / 2g. (recommended)

Cooking instructions:
Preheat the oven to 250 degrees Celsius and bake the hot peppers until the bowl becomes dark (about 20 minutes). Cover the hot peppers with a clear film and allow to cool. Peel the skin and cut into strips about 2 cm wide. Cut tomatoes in half and spread with oil in slices of aubergine and bake in the oven at 200 degrees golden brown (about 10 minutes) Fry the zucchini slices in the grill pan (without fat).
Mix everything together, mix the marinade of olive oil, salt and lemon peel and pour over the vegetables, sprinkle with coriander. Leave for 1 hour.

9.3   Asparagus and herb ragout

Diuretic, improves blood circulation, prevents cancer, dissolves stagnation, promotes weight loss. Good to fight immunodeficiency, loss of appetite, flatulence, high blood pressure, depressions, diabetes, diarrhea, stimulates liver function.
Cooking time approx. 30 min
Calories p. portion: 168
4 portions
Allergens: GL

Quantity of ingredients:
Basic recipe for a vegetable soup (nutritious) 2 cups / 500g. (recommended)
Lemon peel 1/2 piece / 3g. (yes)
Coriander 1/4 teaspoon / 1g. (recommended)
Nutmeg 1 pinch / 0,3g. (recommended)
Asparagus (green or white) 1,8 lbs / 800g. (recommended)
Parsley 1 Bunch / 125g. (recommended)
Créme fraiche cheese 2 table spoons / 30g. ()
Lemon juice 1 teaspoon / 3g. (yes)
Potato 7/8 lbs / 400g. (recommended)

Cooking instructions:
Cook potatoes with plenty of salted water about 20 min. until soft.
Heat the vegetable stock with lemon zest, coriander and nutmeg till it boil. Cook the peeled and sliced asparagus in it.
Drain asparagus in a sieve. Collect the cooking liquid.
In the blender mix 200 g of cooked asparagus (the lower ends), cooking liquid and parsley to a smooth sauce. Beat the sauce with crème fraiche until smooth. Add asparagus and heat again and season with lemon juice, salt and pepper. Serve with the potatoes.

9.4   Basic recipe for a beef broth (clear)

Strengthens muscles, tendons and bones, reduces blood pressure, strengthens immune system, prevents cancer, reduces radiation damage, stimulates digestion, reduces pain, promotes digestion, diuretic. Rosemary stimulates digestion.
Cooking time approx. 4-8 hours
Calories p. portion: 114
10 portions
Allergens: O

Quantity of ingredients:
Beef soup meat 1,1 lbs / 500g. (little)
Beef meatbones 5/8 oz / 200g. (little)
Vinegar (Red wine vinegar) 1 dash / 3g. (yes)
Juniper berry 8 pieces / 6g. (recommended)
Rosemary 1 pinch / 1g. (yes)
Carrot 3 pieces / 210g. (recommended)
Parsnip 2 pieces / 300g. (recommended)
Leek 1 piece / 200g. (yes)

Ginger fresh 1/2 teaspoon / 5g. (recommended)
Lovage 1 stem / 15g. (recommended)
Clove 2 pieces / 2g. (recommended)
Pimento 6 pieces / 12g. (yes)
Anise (Common Fennel) 2 pieces / 1g. (recommended)
Salt 1 teaspoon / 5g. (little)
Water 3,3 lbs / 1300g. (yes)

Cooking instructions:
Heat water, a dash of red wine vinegar, some juniper berries, a little
rosemary, bones and meat till it boils; add carrot, parsnip, leek, ginger,
lovage, clove, allspice, star anise and a little salt; simmer for 4-8 hours
then strain. Refrigerate for later use.

9.5 Basic recipe for a fish broth

Strengthens the kidneys, promotes watering, reduces blood pressure,
strengthens immune system, prevents cancer, reduces radiation
damage. Low in cholesterol and protein rich. Improves blood circulation,
stimulates appetite.
Cooking time approx. 40 min
Calories p. portion: 128
5 portions
Allergens: DLO

Quantity of ingredients:
Fish pieces mixed (fresh water) 3/4 lbs / 300g. (yes)
Celery root 1/4 lbs - 4oz / 120g. (recommended)
Leek 2 inches / 10g. (yes)
Carrot 2 pieces / 150g. (recommended)
White wine 1/2 cup / 125g. (yes)
Lemon 1/2 piece / 50g. (yes)
Bay leaf 2 leaves / 2g. (recommended)
Peppercorns 3 pieces / 2g. (yes)
Olive oil 1 table spoon / 10g. (recommended)
Water 2 cup / 450g. (yes)

Cooking instructions:
Fry celery, chopped carrots and leeks in olive oil, add bay leaf and
peppercorns, add pieces of fish and sauté briefly. Add water, add little
white wine or lemon. Simmer gently for 30 minutes. Skim off the
resulting foam several times. In the end, sift the ingredients through a
cloth. Refrigerate for later use

9.6 Basic recipe for a vegetable soup, nutritious

Reduces blood pressure, strengthens immune system, prevents cancer, forcing spleen, dissolves stagnation, promotes weight loss. Good to fight immunodeficiency, high blood pressure, depressions, diabetes, diarrhea, reduces blood lipids.
Cooking time approx. 2-3 hours
Calories p. portion: 48
5 portions
Allergens: L

Quantity of ingredients:
Olive oil 1 table spoon / 4g. (recommended)
Onion white 1 piece / 60g. (yes)
Carrot 3 pieces / 200g. (recommended)
Parsnip 3/8 lbs - 6oz / 150g. (recommended)
Celery root 1 cup / 100g. (recommended)
Ginger fresh 1/2 teaspoon / 2g. (recommended)
Lemon 1/2 piece / 25g. (yes)
Juniper berry 6 pieces / 6g. (recommended)
Thyme dried 1 pinch / 1g. (recommended)
Lovage 1 table spoon / 3g. (recommended)
Bay leaf 2 leaves / 1g. (recommended)
Salt 1 pinch / 1g. (little)
Water 3 cups / 650g. (yes)

Cooking instructions:
Cut the vegetables into cubes.
Heat oil in hot pot, fry shortly onions and vegetables.
Add cold water, then add ginger, bay leaf and lemon juice.
Season with juniper, thyme and lovage. Cover for 2 - 3 hours on a low heat and simmer.
The used vegetables should be thrown away.
The basic recipe serves as a soup base and to refine vegetables, legumes or cereals.
If you want to eat vegetable soup immediately, add the desired vegetables half an hour before.
Refrigerate for later use.

9.7   Basmati rice + Zucchini tofu dish

Diuretic, supports urination, harmonizes spleen and stomach, reduces flatulence, good to fight body overweight and high blood pressure. Antioxidativ, promotes digestion, perspiration, reduces blood lipids, forcing spleen.
Cooking time approx. 20 min
Calories p. portion: 146
4 portions
Allergens: E

Quantity of ingredients:
Soy Tofu 5/8 lbs - 8oz / 250g. (yes)
Olive oil 2 table spoons / 6g. (recommended)
Coriander 1/2 teaspoon / 4g. (recommended)
Ginger fresh 1/2 teaspoon / 4g. (recommended)
Rice Basmati 1/2 cup / 60g. (yes)
Water 3 cups / 200g. (yes)
Zucchini 1 piece / 700g. (recommended)

Cooking instructions:
Cut tofu cubes and marinate with olive oil, tamari, crushed coriander and ginger. Leave at least 1 hour.

Cook Basmati rice with the water. You can season with onion and cardamom.
Roast zucchini and tofu in pan in the hot oil for approx. 5-7 min.
Serve rice and tofu on a plate.
Add the parsley.

Can also be used as a salad for the home and on the go.

9.8   Bean paste piquant sweet

Supports urination, lowers cholesterol, prevents arteriosclerosis, antioxidativ. Promotes digestion, helps to digest fat, supports urination, reduces blood pressure.
Cooking time approx. 1 hour
Calories p. portion: 311
1 portions
Allergens: MO

Quantity of ingredients:
Black beans 1 cup / 120g. (yes)
Ginger fresh 1 inch / 3g. (recommended)
Boxhorn clover seeds 1/2 teaspoon / 2g. (yes)
Tomato paste 1 table spoon / 10g. (recommended)
Olive oil 2 table spoons / 20g. (recommended)
Pumpkin seed oil 1 dash / 3g. (yes)
Mustard 1 knife tip / 1g. (yes)
Radish horseradish 1 teaspoon (grated) / 2g. (recommended)
Pepper (ground) 1 pinch / 0,5g. (yes)
Garlic 2 cloves / 3g. (recommended)
Salt 1 pinch / 1g. (little)
Sugar molasses 2 table spoons / 20g. (little)
Lemon peel 1/2 piece / 1g. (yes)

Cooking instructions:
Boil beans (with spices and ginger), drain water and puree. Season with spices.

Refine with sugar beet syrup and lemon peel.

9.9   Beluga lentil stew with vegetables

Promotes sweating, dissolves stagnation. Relieves constipation, strengthens mother milk production, stimulates nerves, detoxifying, reduces inflammation, improves blood circulation. Strengthens heart and kidney, diuretic, calms the stomach, promotes digestion.
Cooking time approx. 20 min
Calories p. portion: 201
5 portions
Allergens:

Quantity of ingredients:
Lentils 1 1/2 cups / 240g. (yes)
Water 4-5 cups / 500g. (yes)
Carrot 3 pieces / 150g. (recommended)
Leek 1 piece / 300g. (yes)
Kohlrabi 1/2 piece / 200g. (yes)
Tomato 2 pieces / 80g. (recommended)
Onion white 1 piece / 50g. (yes)
Bay leaf 2 leaves / 1g. (recommended)
Fennel 1 piece / 250g. (recommended)
Star anise 2 pieces / 1g. (yes)

Juniper berry 6 pieces / 2g. (recommended)
Olive oil 2 table spoons / 30g. (recommended)
Salt 1 pinch / 1g. (little)
Ginger fresh 1/2 teaspoon / 2g. (recommended)
Black caraway 1 pinch / 1g. (yes)

Cooking instructions:
Heat oil in hot pot. Fry onions and add diced vegetables and spices, lentils (washed well) and salt. Cover with cold water (3 fingers wide) and cook for 20 minutes on a low heat.
Sprinkle with fresh herbs and black cumin

Goes well with rice!

9.10 Black root with yogurt

Stimulates kidney, bladder and forces the cleaning of the body. In the physiological sense, they generally stimulate the glands in the organism. Good to fight acute or chronic constipation of the intestine. Rich in Vitamins and trace elements.
Cooking time approx. 20 min
Calories p. portion: 424
2 portions
Allergens: AG

Quantity of ingredients:
Salsify 1 lbs / 400g. (recommended)
Yogurt (natural, 1.5% fat) 4 table spoons / 80g. (recommended)
Herbs various 1 table spoon / 8g. (yes)
Salt 1 pinch / 1g. (little)
Herbs various 2 table spoons / 6g. (yes)
Multi-grain bread (gray bread) 6 slices / 120g. (yes)

Cooking instructions:
Peel the salsify and simmer in salted water until tender. Pour away the water, cool the salsify and cut it to size.
Cover with yoghurt and sprinkle with fresh herbs. Serve with the bread. You can also use the salsify from the conserve.

9.11 Broccoli cream soup

Strengthen your immune system, build and maintain healthy bones, teeth, hair and nails. Reduces blood pressure, strengthens immune system, prevents cancer, reduces radiation damage.
Cooking time approx. 30 min
Calories p. portion: 98
6 portions
Allergens: LO

Quantity of ingredients:
Olive oil 2 table spoons / 7g. (recommended)
Broccoli 1,1 lbs / 500g. (recommended)
Carrot 2 pieces / 150g. (recommended)
Potato 2 pieces / 120g. (recommended)
Onion white 1 piece / 50g. (yes)
Water 1 cup / 50g. (yes)
Basic recipe for a vegetable soup (nutritious) 2 cup / 500g. (recommended)
White wine 1/2 cup / 125g. (yes)
Sage 1 teaspoon / 2g. (recommended)
Rosemary 1 teaspoon / 2g. (yes)
Pepper (ground) 1 pinch / 0,5g. (yes)
Salt 1 pinch / 1g. (little)

Cooking instructions:
Add the olive oil to the pan, add the washed and cut broccoli, diced carrots and potatoes, sauté for a short time, add the chopped onion, fill with water, enough water to cover the vegetables at least 3 finger breadths. Add bouillon, salt, add a little bit of white wine, add the seasoned sage and rosemary.
Heat till it boils and then simmer on a small fire for about 25 minutes. Season with pepper, if necessary season with sea salt. Purée the soup.

9.12 Bulgur with tomatoes and fresh herbs

Promotes digestion, helps to digest fat, supports urination, reduces blood pressure. Stimulates digestion, supports urination.
Cooking time approx. 30 min
Calories p. portion: 205
1 portions
Allergens: A

Quantity of ingredients:
Bulgur (cereals) 1 cup / 120g. (yes)
Tomato 2 pieces / 70g. (recommended)
Rucola 2 table spoons / 16g. (recommended)
Pepper powder (hot) 1 pinch / 2g. (yes)
Olive oil 2 table spoons / 20g. (recommended)
Pepper (ground) 1 pinch / 0,5g. (yes)
Salt 1 pinch / 1g. (little)
Basil 4 leaves / 2g. (yes)
Thyme 1 Twig / 3g. (yes)
Lemon juice 1/2 piece / 10g. (yes)

Cooking instructions:
Put cold water in a pot, sprinkle in Bulgur and simmer. Stir in chopped tomatoes, fresh herbs like basil, thyme, arugula, a pinch of rose paprika, lemon juice, a dash of olive oil, a little ground pepper, some salt.

Variant: add some mozzarella.

Recommendation: ideal morning meal in summer; also suitable as evening meal, especially for sleep disorders.

9.13 Carrot and potato rucola sandwich

Reduces inflammation, improves digestion, supports urination, lowers cholesterol, strengthens immune system, prevents cancer, good to fight constipation (Fibre-rich), dissolves stagnation.
Cooking time approx. 20 min
Calories p. portion: 94
4 portions
Allergens: AG

Quantity of ingredients:
Potato (mealy) 5/8 oz / 200g. (recommended)
Carrot 1 piece / 50g. (recommended)
Sour cream 15% fat 2 table spoons / 45g. (yes)
Onion (spring onion) 1 piece / 20g. (yes)
Rucola 1/2 bunch / 100g. (recommended)
Lemon peel 1/4 teaspoon / 1g. (yes)
Salt 1 pinch / 1g. (little)
Pepper (ground) 1 pinch / 0,2g. (yes)
Whole grain bread 8 slices / 48g. (recommended)

Cooking instructions:
Cook the potatoes gently, peel and squeeze through the potato press.
Cook vegetable broth according to the basic recipe and remove a carrot after a short cooking time and finely crush with a fork.
Stir the potatoes, carrots, grated lemon zest and sour cream into a smooth cream.
Mix carrot and potato cream with finely chopped rocket salad. Season the spread with salt and pepper and spread the bread. Sprinkle with the finely chopped young onions.

9.14 Celery and potato cream soup

Reduces blood pressure, strengthens immune system, promotes weight loss. Good to fight immunodeficiency, loss of appetite, flatulence, depressions, diabetes, diarrhea, improves digestion.
Cooking time approx. 45 min
Calories p. portion: 113
4 portions
Allergens: GL

Quantity of ingredients:
Olive oil 1 table spoon / 10g. (recommended)
Onion white 1/2 piece / 25g. (yes)
Basic recipe for a vegetable soup (nutritious) 3 cups / 700g. (recommended)
Potato 5/8 oz / 200g. (recommended)
Nutmeg 1 pinch / 0,5g. (recommended)
Ground 1 pinch / 0,5g. (yes)
Lemon peel 1/4 piece / 1g. (yes)
Créme fraiche cheese 2 table spoons / 20g. ()
Salt 1 pinch / 1g. (little)
Parsley 1 table spoon / 8g. (recommended)

Cooking instructions:
Heat the olive oil in a saucepan lightly. Fry the onions very gently in a mild heat. Pour with vegetable stock according to the basic recipe. Cover and cook for 15 minutes.
Add curd-cut potato, celery, nutmeg, cumin and lemon zest. Spice with salt and cook for 12 minutes. Potatoes and celery should be soft. Remove the lemon peel.
Puree the soup with crème fraiche using a blender. Season the soup with salt.
Arrange the soup in portions with the chopped parsley.

9.15 Champignon rice

Strengthens kidney, diuretic, warming the body from the inside, expands blood vessels, strengthens the muscles, promotes digestion and is good to fight high blood pressure, dissolves stagnation, promotes weight loss. Good to fight immunodeficiency, loss of appetite.
Cooking time approx. 30 min
Calories p. portion: 410
2 portions
Allergens: L

Quantity of ingredients:
Onion white 1 piece / 50g. (yes)
Bay leaf 2 pieces / 1g. (recommended)
Clove 2 pieces / 1g. (recommended)
Basic recipe for a vegetable soup (nutritious) 7/8 lbs / 350g. (recommended)
Rice (whole grain) 5/8 oz / 200g. (recommended)
Champignon 1/8 lbs - 2oz / 60g. (yes)
Parsley 1/2 oz / 20g. (recommended)
Pepper (ground) 1 pinch / 0,2g. (yes)

Cooking instructions:
Plug in the cloves in the onion. Heat the vegetable stock with the onion and the bay leaves till it boils. Add the rice to the boiling liquid, reduce the temperature to the lowest level and stir with the lid closed for 20-25 minutes.
In the meantime, wash the mushrooms, clean them, slice them, sauté briefly with a little water or sauté. Wash the parsley and chop finely. Remove the onion from the rice, add the mushrooms and the parsley, season with pepper.

9.16 Chicory salad with oranges and grapefruit

Mineral supporter and is full of A-B-C vitamins. Promotes digestion, relieves alcohol poisoning, lowers blood glucose. Promotes digestion.
Cooking time approx. 10 min
Calories p. portion: 236
1 portions
Allergens:

Quantity of ingredients:
Chicory 1/4 lbs - 4oz / 120g. (recommended)
Orange 1 piece / 100g. (yes)
Grapefruit (Pomelo) 1/2 piece / 100g. (yes)
Onion white 1 smal / 30g. (yes)
Lemon juice 2 table spoons / 20g. (yes)
Pepper (ground) 1 pinch / 0,2g. (yes)
Ginger powder 1 pinch / 0,2g. (yes)
Sugar candy white 1 knife tip / 0,5g. (little)
Orange grated peel 1 teaspoon / 2g. (recommended)
Olive oil 1 table spoon / 10g. (recommended)

Cooking instructions:
Wash chicory and cut it to size. Peel and fillet oranges and grapefruit.
Mix with the chicory. From lemon juice, salt, pepper, ginger, sugar,
chopped onion and oil stir a sauce. Mix chicory, orange fillets and
sauce. Sprinkle the salad with orange peel rasps.

9.17 Colorful rice dish

Strengthens immune system, strengthens the muscles, tendons and
bones, promotes digestion, helps to digest fat, supports urination,
reduces blood pressure, dissolves stagnation.
Cooking time approx. 45 min
Calories p. portion: 437
3 portions
Allergens: L

Quantity of ingredients:
Olive oil 2 teaspoons / 20g. (recommended)
Onion (spring onion) 1 piece / 20g. (yes)
Beef meat 1/4 lbs - 4oz / 125g. (little)
Rice (whole grain) 3 oz / 80g. (recommended)
Basic recipe for a vegetable soup 1 cup / 300g. (recommended)
Celery root 1/8 lbs - 2oz / 50g. (recommended)
Leek 1 piece / 100g. (yes)
Beans (green, fresh) 3/8 lbs - 6oz / 150g. (recommended)
Carrot 1 piece / 70g. (recommended)
Tomato 2 pieces / 100g. (recommended)
Salt 1 pinch / 0,5g. (little)
Pepper (ground) 1 pinch / 0,2g. (yes)
Peppers powder 1 pinch / 0,5g. (yes)
Herbs various 2 table spoons / 12g. (yes)

Cooking instructions:
Wash leek and carrots, clean and chop them. Dice the celery, slice the tomatoes.

Fry in a large, deep pan with oil, onion and minced meat.

Add brown rice and prepared vegetables (celery, leeks, beans, carrots, tomatoes). Braise briefly.

Season with salt, pepper and paprika. Add vegetable broth. Heat till it boils and cook over low heat for 20 to 30 minutes with the lid closed.

Sprinkle with fresh chopped herbs and serve.

9.18 Colorful tuscan bean soup

Promotes digestion, helps to digest fat, supports urination, reduces blood pressure, diuretic, calms the stomach.
Cooking time approx. 2 hours
Calories p. portion: 249
3 portions
Allergens: L

Quantity of ingredients:
Kidney beans (red) 1/8 lbs - 2oz / 50g. (yes)
Chickpeas 1 oz / 25g. (yes)
Lentils 1 oz / 25g. (yes)
Celery sticks 1 stick / 10g. (recommended)
Tomato 2 pieces / 100g. (recommended)
Fennel seeds ground 1/2 teaspoon / 1g. (yes)
Salt 1 pinch / 1g. (little)
Pepper (ground) 1 pinch / 0,5g. (yes)
Garlic 1 clove / 3g. (recommended)
Olive oil 2 table spoons / 50g. (recommended)
Water 2 1/4 cups / 500g. (yes)
Basil (fresh) 5-7 leaves / 3g. (recommended)

Cooking instructions:
Soak legumes, boil and puree. Add vegetables, spices, herbs and oil and cook gently for 2 hours.

Variation: Sweet chestnuts give the dish a special Italian touch.

9.19 Compote from apples

Apple (sweet) stops diarrhea, promotes digestion, appetizing, harmonizes the stomach. Warms stomach and spleen, improves blood circulation.
Cooking time approx. 10 min
Calories p. portion: 67
2 portions
Allergens:

Quantity of ingredients:
Apple (sweet) 1 piece / 220g. (recommended)
Water 1 1/2 cups / 220g. (yes)
Cinnamon ground 1 pinch / 1g. (recommended)

Cooking instructions:
Cook the apples (organic) with the skin and seeds. Sprinkle with cinnamon.

9.20 Compote from blueberries

Laxative, antibacterial effect. Warms stomach and spleen, improves blood circulation.
Cooking time approx. 10 min
Calories p. portion: 49
1 portions
Allergens:

Quantity of ingredients:
Blueberry 1/4 lbs - 4oz / 100g. (recommended)
Water 1 cup / 120g. (yes)
Cinnamon ground 1 pinch / 0,1g. (recommended)
Lemon peel 1 pinch / 1g. (yes)
Sugar cane sugar 1 teaspoon / 3g. (little)

Cooking instructions:
Cook the blueberries gently and sprinkle with sugar, cinnamon and grated lemon zest.

9.21 Couscous Salad

prevents cancer, forcing spleen, promotes digestion, stimulates liver function, reduces blood pressure, strengthens immune system, reduces radiation damage, diuretic.
Cooking time approx. 25 min
Calories p. portion: 338
3 portions
Allergens: A

Quantity of ingredients:
Water 1 cup / 100g. (yes)
Olive oil 1 table spoon / 15g. (recommended)
Couscous 5/8 oz / 200g. (yes)
Lemon juice 2 table spoons / 30g. (yes)
Lemon peel 1 teaspoon / 2g. (yes)
Tomato 2 pieces / 80g. (recommended)
Cucumber 1/4 lbs - 4oz / 100g. (yes)
Carrot 1/4 lbs - 4oz / 100g. (recommended)
Parsley 1 Bunch / 100g. (recommended)
Chives 1 Bunch / 100g. (recommended)
Peppermint 3 twigs / 30g. (recommended)

Cooking instructions:
Boil in a small saucepan 250 ml. water with salt and 1 tablespoon olive oil. Add the couscous, take the stove in the front and let it swell covered for 5 minutes. Put the couscous back on the stove and let it simmer for about 2 minutes with gentle stirring. If necessary, add 1 - 3 tbsp of hot water.
Mix the couscous with lemon juice, chopped lemon peel and 1 tbsp oil, season with salt and pepper and leave to set.
Add couscous with tomatoes, cucumber, parsley (all diced), carrots (grated), chives and mint (finely chopped).
Season the couscous salad with lemon juice, salt and pepper.

9.22 Cream cheese substitute

Good to fight lactose intolerance, promotes digestion. Good to fight immunodeficiency, loss of appetite, arteriosclerosis, flatulence, bladder weakness, anemia, high blood pressure, diabetes, diarrhea.
Cooking time approx. 20 min
Calories p. portion: 526
2 portions
Allergens: AE

Quantity of ingredients:
Soybean milk 4 cup / 300g. (yes)
Lemon 1 piece / 50g. (yes)
Herbs various 2 table spoons / 6g. (yes)
Whole grain bread 6 slices / 300g. (recommended)

Cooking instructions:
Heat the soy milk in a saucepan till it boils, stirring occasionally (gets burn easily!), Then allow to cool.
Squeeze out the lemon and stir gently under the cooled soy milk (approx. 80°C/176°F), let it approx. 20 min. rest or clot.
Pour chopped soy milk through a strainer lined with a dishcloth, allow liquid to drain and then squeeze out remaining liquid with the dishcloth.
Refine to taste with fresh herbs. Serve with wholemeal bread.

9.23 Cucumber salad

Diuretic, detoxifying, suppresses conversion of sugar into fat, lowers cholesterol, prevents cancer. Cucumber cools and moistens. Dill works against flatulence, anticonvulsant in gastrointestinal discomfort.
Cooking time approx. 5 min
Calories p. portion: 27
2 portions
Allergens: O

Quantity of ingredients:
Cucumber 1 piece / 400g. (yes)
Salt 1 pinch / 1g. (little)
Dill 1 pinch / 1g. (recommended)
Vinegar (Apple vinegar) 1 table spoon / 10g. (recommended)

Cooking instructions:
Cut the cucumber (do not peel the BIO) thinly and season.

9.24 Cucumber soup

Diuretic, detoxifying, suppresses conversion of sugar into fat, lowers cholesterol, prevents cancer, promotes digestion, diaphoretic, dries out, good to fight yeast infections.
Cooking time approx. 20 min
Calories p. portion: 96
4 portions
Allergens: M

Quantity of ingredients:
Olive oil 2 table spoons / 35g. (recommended)
Cucumber 2 pieces / 400g. (yes)
Water 2 cup / 500g. (yes)
Sage 3 leaves / 3g. (recommended)
Mustard 1/2 teaspoon / 0,5g. (yes)
Coriander 1 pinch / 1g. (recommended)
Cardamom 1 pinch / 1g. (recommended)
Salt 1 pinch / 1g. (little)

Cooking instructions:
Heat oil and roast short the small cucumbers. Add Mustard seeds,
coriander, cardamom and salt. Add water.
Simmer for 10-15 min. Puree and decorate with fresh chopped sage.

9.25 Delicately spiced zucchini with tomatoes

Diuretic, promotes digestion, helps to digest fat, reduces blood
pressure, dissolves stagnation, antioxidativ, supports urination, diuretic,
warming the body from the inside, expands blood vessels.
Cooking time approx. 10 min
Calories p. portion: 203
4 portions
Allergens:

Quantity of ingredients:
Olive oil 1 table spoon / 20g. (recommended)
Onion white 2 pieces / 120g. (yes)
Zucchini 4 pieces / 800g. (recommended)
Oregano dried 1 pinch / 1g. (recommended)
Basil (fresh) 6-8 leaves / 3g. (recommended)
Salt 1 pinch / 1g. (little)
Tomato 2 pieces / 120g. (recommended)
Rice (whole grain) 1 cup / 120g. (recommended)
Water 6 cups / 400g. (yes)
Salt 1 pinch / 1g. (little)

Cooking instructions:
In a hot pan, fry olive oil, finely chopped onions and finely chopped zucchini until half cooked. Add plenty of dried oregano. Salt and chop the tomatoes for a few minutes until the zucchini are tender but crisp. Add fresh basil as desired.

Variation: Put some sheep's cheese over the tomatoes and finish cooking with the lid closed.

Place the rice in salted water, heat till it boils and let it simmer over low heat for about 15 minutes.

9.26 Exotic lenses

Strengthens heart and kidney, diuretic, calms the stomach, promotes digestion, dissolves stagnation, helps to digest fat, supports urination, reduces blood pressure, detoxifying and stimulating the immune system.
Cooking time approx. 45 min
Calories p. portion: 144
4 portions
Allergens: NO

Quantity of ingredients:
Sesame oil 1 table spoon / 10g. (little)
Onion white 2 pieces / 120g. (yes)
Ginger fresh 1/2 teaspoon / 2g. (recommended)
Thyme dried 1/2 teaspoon / 1g. (recommended)
Cumin (Caraway seed) 1/2 teaspoon / 2g. (recommended)
Lentils red 1 cup / 120g. (yes)
Wakame 1 inch / 1g. (recommended)
Lemon 1/2 piece / 20g. (yes)
Bocksdorn fruits (Fructus Lycii, Goji, 2 pinches / 2g. (yes)
Sugar cane sugar 1 pinch / 1g. (little)
Salt 1 pinch / 1g. (little)
Vinegar (Apple vinegar) 1/2 teaspoon / 1g. (recommended)
Tomato 1 piece / 50g. (recommended)
Chard 5/8 oz / 200g. (recommended)
Cauliflower 5/8 oz / 200g. (yes)
Salt 1 pinch / 1g. (little)
Rice (whole grain) 1/2 cup / 60g. (recommended)
Water 3 cups / 300g. (yes)
Salt 1 pinch / 1g. (little)

Cooking instructions:
Heat sesame oil in a hot pot. Add chopped onions, grated ginger, dried thyme, plenty of cumin and sauté gently.
Add peeled red lentils, a strip of wakame, a little lemon juice, hot water and some dried buckthorn fruits. Simmer for 20 minutes until the lentils are cooked; add hot water as needed to make a pulp. Add sugar, some chili and salt.
Add vinegar or lemon juice depending on your taste. Add chopped tomatoes as desired. Let it pass for a few minutes.

Cook in a small pot with 1 cup of water and a little salt the cauliflower 10 min. until soft.

Blanch in a small pot with 1 cup of water and salt the chard 3 min.
Boil the rice briefly, salt and 10 min. to let go. Serve everything with the lentil dish.

9.27 Fine Russian borscht

Strengths spleen and stomach, strengthens the heart, stimulates digestion, reduces blood pressure, strengthens immune system. For strengthening after diseases. Good to fight bloating, cramping in gastrointestinal complaints.
Cooking time approx. 30 min
Calories p. portion: 172
6 portions
Allergens: AGLO

Quantity of ingredients:
Red beet 5/8 oz / 200g. (recommended)
Sunflower oil 1 table spoon / 10g. (little)
Onion (shallot) 2 pieces / 40g. (yes)
Carrot 2 pieces / 140g. (recommended)
Celery root 1 piece / 500g. (recommended)
Parsley root 1 piece / 150g. (yes)
Leek 1/8 lbs - 2oz / 50g. (yes)
Basic recipe for a vegetable soup 3 cups / 650g. (recommended)
Bay leaf 1 Leaf / 0,2g. (recommended)
Juniper berry 2 pieces / 2g. (recommended)
Nutmeg 1 pinch / 1g. (recommended)
Savoy cabbage / kale 5/8 oz / 200g. (yes)
Salt 1 pinch / 1g. (little)

Pepper (ground) 1 pinch / 0,5g. (yes)
Ground 1 pinch / 1g. (yes)
Red wine 1/2 cup / 125g. (yes)
Sour cream 15% fat 1 table spoon / 10g. (yes)
Dill 1 teaspoon / 10g. (recommended)
White bread (wheat bread) 6 slices / 120g. (little)

Cooking instructions:
Fry some beetroot in oil. Fry the onions, carrots, celery, parsley root and leek well in another pan. Add the stock and the wine; then add bay leaves, juniper berries and nutmeg and simmer for 15 minutes. Remove the bay leaf and puree everything.
Heat more broth separately, simmer the steamed beetroot in it. Add cabbage or white cabbage after half the cooking time and let it steep. At the end, add the pureed vegetables and season with salt, pepper, ground cumin and a little red wine. Garnish with some sour cream and finely chopped dill in the plate. Serve with a slice of white bread.

9.28 Fish soup with white wine, laurel and marjoram

Strengthens the kidneys, promotes watering, promotes spleen and liver, reduces blood pressure, improves blood circulation, improves medication effect, stimulates appetite, reduces blood pressure.
Cooking time approx. 45 min
Calories p. portion: 200
3 portions
Allergens: DLO

Quantity of ingredients:
Onion (spring onion) 2 pieces / 40g. (yes)
Garlic 1 clove / 2g. (recommended)
Basic recipe for a fish soup 2 cup / 500g. (yes)
Carrot 1 piece / 60g. (recommended)
Parsnip 1 piece / 100g. (recommended)
Celery root 1 slice / 60g. (recommended)
Salt 1 pinch / 1g. (little)
Peppercorns 2 pieces / 1g. (yes)
Lemon 1/4 piece / 10g. (yes)
White wine 1/2 cup / 125g. (yes)
Bay leaf 2 leaves / 1g. (recommended)
Rosemary 1 teaspoon / 2g. (yes)
Chives 1 teaspoon (chopped) / 3g. (recommended)
Parsley 1 teaspoon (chopped) / 3g. (recommended)

Cooking instructions:
Fry the onion and garlic in oil until translucent. Add fish broth. Add the diced carrot, parsnip and celery. Season with salt and peppercorns. Simmer the soup on a low heat for 25 minutes.
Wash the fish, drizzle with lemon juice, divide into pieces and add to the soup with the wine, the bay leaves and the marjoram. Cook for 5 min on low heat.
Add the chives and parsley and season the soup with the salt.

9.29 Fried asparagus with rocket

Diuretic, improves blood circulation, prevents cancer, stimulates digestion, forcing spleen, promotes weight loss. Good to fight immunodeficiency, loss of appetite, arteriosclerosis, flatulence, bladder weakness, anemia, high blood pressure, depressions, diabetes.
Cooking time approx. 15 min
Calories p. portion: 149
3 portions
Allergens: G

Quantity of ingredients:
Butter organic 1 table spoon / 20g. ()
Asparagus (green or white) 1,1 lbs / 500g. (recommended)
Pepper (ground) 1 pinch / 0,5g. (yes)
Salt 1 pinch / 1g. (little)
Lemon 1/4 piece / 12g. (yes)
Rucola 2 handful / 30g. (recommended)
Potato 3/4 lbs / 300g. (recommended)

Cooking instructions:
Melt a piece of butter in a hot pan; cut the peeled asparagus into pieces of 3 to 4 cm, fry for about 10 minutes until tender, but crisp. Sprinkle with freshly ground pepper, salt, add a few drops of lemon juice or finely grated lemon zest, finely shredded rucola leaves.
Cook the potatoes in plenty of salted water, then peel.

9.30 Grilled salmon steaks with cauliflower and potatoes

Improves digestion, regenerates skin, supports urination, lowers cholesterol, supports digestion.
Cooking time approx. 30 min
Calories p. portion: 330
4 portions
Allergens: D

Quantity of ingredients:
Garlic 1 clove / 1g. (recommended)
Onion (shallot) 1/2 piece / 5g. (yes)
Lemon juice 1 dash / 1g. (yes)
Salt 1 pinch / 1g. (little)
Cauliflower 1 piece / 500g. (yes)
Olive oil 2 table spoons / 20g. (recommended)
Garlic 1 clove / 1g. (recommended)
Water 2/3 cup / g. (yes)
Parsley 2 table spoons / 15g. (recommended)
Potato 1,1 lbs / 500g. (recommended)
Salt 1 pinch / 1g. (little)
Salmon 4 pieces (steaks) / 500g. (recommended)
Lemon 1/2 piece / 2g. (yes)

Cooking instructions:
Garlic shallots mixture:
Finely squeeze the garlic, finely chop the shallots, add a dash of lemon juice and salt and stir. Mix with a little oil to a paste.

Cauliflower:
Cut the cauliflower into pieces.
Heat the oil in a heavy saucepan and fry the crushed garlic for a short time.
Add the cauliflower pieces and turn in the oil. Add a little water and cook until the cauliflower is firm. Strain the cauliflower and cook the remaining water until a thick sauce remains. Add the cauliflower and crush it roughly with a wooden spoon. Add the chopped parsley and salt.

Potatoes:
Cook the potato in a saucepan with plenty of water, strain and peel.

Salmon Steak:
Preheat the oven at about 180°C/356°F. Rub in the salmon slices with the garlic-scarlet mixture and grill as close as possible to the heat source for 4 to 8 minutes from both sides. You are done when the meat is easy to divide when you pierce with a fork.

Serve and sprinkle with lemon slices and the chopped parsley.

9.31 Grilled tofu with rice noodles, spinach and sugar snaps

Reduces flatulence. Supports urination, detoxifying. Good to fight blood circulation disorders. Strengthens gastrointestinal function, expands blood vessels, stimulates appetite. Promotes bowel movement, improves blood circulation.
Cooking time approx. 30 min
Calories p. portion: 327
4 portions
Allergens: E

Quantity of ingredients:
Sake 1/3 cup / 85g. (little)
Sugar cane sugar 1 table spoon / 7g. (little)
Garlic 5 cloves / 7g. (recommended)
Onion (spring onion) 3 pieces / 60g. (yes)
Ginger fresh 1 inch / 5g. (recommended)
Rapeseed oil 2 table spoons / 20g. (recommended)
Spinach 2 handful / 30g. (yes)
Peas, green 7/8 lbs / 400g. (recommended)
Water 1 table spoon / g. (yes)
Rice noodles 1 package / 250g. (yes)
Water 4 cup / g. (yes)
Basil 1 table spoon / 3g. (yes)
Soy Tofu 1,1 lbs / 500g. (yes)

Cooking instructions:
In a medium bowl mix together: Tamari souce, rice wine, sugar, crushed garlic, spring onion, grated ginger, chopped basil and the rapeseed oil. Add the tofu and leave in the marinade for at least 1 hour. Cover the mangetout peas in a pan with a little water, lightly simmer 5 min. Add the spinach and steam again 3 min.

Cook the rice noodles according to manufacturer's instructions, drain, rinse again with warm water and drain.

Preheat the grill or oven grill, grill the tofu for 5 minutes on both sides and set aside.

Arrange the pasta on the plates, divide the vegetables all around and place the tofu over the noodles. Douse with the marinade.

9.32 Halibut with tomato and garlic sauce

Promotes digestion, helps to digest fat, supports urination, reduces blood pressure, good to fight rheumatism, flatulence, bladder weakness, anemia, high blood pressure, depressions, diabetes, diarrhea. Valuable omega-3 fatty acids.
Cooking time approx. 45 min
Calories p. portion: 319
5 portions
Allergens: D

Quantity of ingredients:
Rice variety any 1 cup / 120g. (yes)
Water 6 cups / 240g. (yes)
Salt 1 pinch / 1g. (little)
Halibut (Flatfish) 2,2 lbs / 800g. (yes)
Salt 1 pinch / 1g. (little)
Pepper (ground) 1 pinch / 0,5g. (yes)
Lemon juice 1 dach / 2g. (yes)
Bay leaf 2 pieces / 2g. (recommended)
Lemon 1 piece / 30g. (yes)
Garlic 8 pieces / 10g. (recommended)
Thyme dried 1 table spoon / 5g. (recommended)
Olives 0,2 lbs / 75g. (yes)
Tomato 4 pieces / 200g. (recommended)
Salt 1 pinch / 1g. (little)
Pepper (ground) 1 pinch / 0,5g. (yes)

Cooking instructions:
Cook rice with salted water (1:3).
Rinse the fish under running cold water, dab with kitchen paper and rub with salt, pepper and lemon juice.
Place the fish fillets in a casserole dish with pieces of bay leaf.

Wash the lemon hot and cut into slices, peel and halve the garlic.
Sprinkle the olives and the thyme over them.
Brew the tomatoes with hot water, skin and chop.

Mix all ingredients, season with salt and pepper and distribute around the fish.

Cook everything at 200°C/392°F for about 20 minutes.
Serve with the rice.

9.33 Hearty polenta mash

Strengths spleen and stomach, promotes watering, promotes digestion, detoxifying, promotes perspiration, reduces blood lipids, stimulates, dissolves stagnation, stimulates appetite, dissolves stagnation.
Cooking time approx. 10 min
Calories p. portion: 262
2 portions
Allergens:

Quantity of ingredients:
Corn Grease (Polenta) 1 cup / 120g. (yes)
Onion (spring onion) 2 pieces / 40g. (yes)
Ginger fresh 1/2 teaspoon / 2g. (recommended)
Nutmeg 1 pinch / 1g. (recommended)
Salt 1 pinch / 1g. (little)
Olive oil 1 table spoon / 10g. (recommended)
Turmeric (yellow root) 1 pinch / 1g. (recommended)
Water 1 1/2 cups / 240g. (yes)

Cooking instructions:
Stir in the polenta in boiling water and let it swell for 7 min. Add green onion, grated ginger, turmeric, nutmeg, salt and olive oil and wait for 3 more minutes.

9.34 Hummus (Chickpeas mash)

Relaxes breast pressure, moisturizer dry skin, helps to fight incontinence, antioxidativ. Stimulates liver function, detoxifying, stimulates the immune system, dissolves stagnation.
Cooking time approx. 2 hours
Calories p. portion: 542
2 portions
Allergens: N

Quantity of ingredients:
Chickpeas 1 1/2 cups / 240g. (yes)
Wakame 1 teaspoon (grated) / 2g. (recommended)
Ginger fresh 1/4 teaspoon / 1g. (recommended)
Rosemary 1 pinch / 0,5g. (yes)
Sesame paste (Tahini) 1 table spoon / 10g. (little)
Olive oil 2 table spoons / 20g. (recommended)
Lemon juice 1 dash / 2g. (yes)
Water upon need / g. (yes)
Garlic 1 clove (scraped) / 2g. (recommended)
Parsley 1 teaspoon (chopped) / 2g. (recommended)
Peppers 1 pinch / 0,2g. (yes)
Curcuma 1 pinch / 0,2g. (yes)
Coriander 1 pinch / 0,2g. (recommended)
Cardamom 1 pinch / 0,2g. (recommended)
Pepper (ground) 1 pinch / 0,2g. (yes)
Salt (herbal) 1/2 teaspoon / 2g. (little)

Cooking instructions:
Soak chickpeas overnight or for at least 6 hours, pour off soaking water, boil in fresh water for about 1 to 1 ½ hours with a little seaweed and ginger, allow to cool.
Seasoning with a few splashes of lemon juice and parsley.
Add the pepper, garlic cut into small pieces or pressed, more or less coriander and cardamom powder, little chilly powder as desired, tahin and olive oil.

Puree all ingredients together. Depending on the consistency, add water. It should be a smooth paste.
Spread on cereal, crackers or toasted bread or enjoy with salad.

9.35 Kohlrabi in chervil sauce with potatoes

Reduces inflammation, lowers cholesterol, diuretic, conducts bowel winds, strengthens immune system, prevents cancer, promotes weight loss. Good to fight loss of appetite, flatulence, high blood pressure, depressions, diabetes, diarrhea.
Cooking time approx. 1 hour
Calories p. portion: 188
4 portions
Allergens: GL

Quantity of ingredients:
Potato 6 pieces / 450g. (recommended)
Basic recipe for a vegetable soup (nutritious) 1 cup / 300g. (recommended)
Potato 1/4 lbs - 4oz / 100g. (recommended)
Nutmeg 1 pinch / 0,2g. (recommended)
Lemon peel 1/2 teaspoon / 2g. (yes)
Ginger fresh 1/2 teaspoon / 2g. (recommended)
Lovage 1/2 teaspoon / 2g. (recommended)
Kohlrabi 3/4 lbs / 300g. (yes)
Salt 1 pinch / 1g. (little)
Pepper (ground) 1 pinch / 0,2g. (yes)
Sour cream 15% fat 2 table spoons / 30g. (yes)
Chervil dried 1 Bunch / 80g. (recommended)

Cooking instructions:
Boil the potatoes in salted water.
Bring half of the vegetable stock to boil. Add the diced potatoes, nutmeg, lemon zest, ginger and lovage. Cover the potatoes and cook for about 10 minutes until soft and puree them with a blender until they are smooth.
Bring remaining vegetable stock to boil. Cut kohlrabi into cubes and add, cover and cook for about 8 minutes. Stir in the potato sauce and heat everything briefly.
Puree with the mixing stick chervil and sour cream. Mix the chervil cream with the kohlrabi vegetables.
Serve with the cooked, peeled potatoes.

9.36 Lentil and chestnut soup with curry

Reduces blood pressure, strengthens immune system, prevents cancer, reduces radiation damage, forcing spleen, dissolves stagnation, promotes weight loss. Good to fight immunodeficiency, loss of appetite, flatulence, high blood pressure, depressions, diabetes, diarrhea.
Cooking time approx. 45 min
Calories p. portion: 176
4 portions
Allergens: LO

Quantity of ingredients:
Lentils red 3/8 lbs - 6oz / 150g. (yes)
Chestnuts 3/8 lbs - 6oz / 150g. (little)
Olive oil 1 table spoon / 10g. (recommended)
Curry 2 teaspoons / 8g. (yes)
Basic recipe for a vegetable soup (nutritious) 2 cup / 500g. (recommended)
Turmeric (yellow root) 1 teaspoon / 2g. (recommended)
White wine 1/2 cup / 125g. (yes)
Salt (herbal) 1 pinch / 1g. (little)
Anise (Common Fennel) 1 pinch / 1g. (recommended)
Cardamom 1 pinch / 0,5g. (recommended)
Cardamom 1 pinch / 1g. (recommended)
Parsley 2 table spoons / 6g. (recommended)

Cooking instructions:
Add the olive oil to a pan, sauté the chestnuts, sprinkle with the curry, add the lentils and season with vegetable stock, add a little white wine, mix in the curcuma, simmer for about 20 minutes (until the chestnuts are tender).
Then puree the soup.
Taste with a pinch of anise, cardamom and herbal salt. At the end, sprinkle finely chopped parsley over it.

9.37 Lentils and rice stew

Promotes spleen and kidney, is very nutritious, reduces blood pressure, strengthens immune system. Good to fight blood circulation disorders, thromboses, risk of embolism, high blood pressure, a headache. Strengthens heart and kidney, diuretic, calms the stomach, promotes digestion.
Cooking time approx. 25 min
Calories p. portion: 232
3 portions
Allergens: LNO

Quantity of ingredients:
Lentils 1/4 lbs - 4oz / 100g. (yes)
Water 5 cups / 500g. (yes)
Rice variety any 1 cup / 120g. (yes)
Sesame oil 1 table spoon / 10g. (little)
Carrot 2 pieces / 150g. (recommended)
Celery sticks 2 rods / 20g. (recommended)

Cumin (Caraway seed) 1 pinch / 0,2g. (recommended)
Salt 1 pinch / 0,5g. (little)
Vinegar (Apple vinegar) 1 dash / 2g. (recommended)
Parsley 2 table spoons / 18g. (recommended)

Cooking instructions:
Soak the dry lentils the day before.
Heat sesame oil in a hot pot; cut carrot and celery into small pieces and
sauté; add rice, a pinch of cumin and lentils and heat till it boils.
If the lenses are soft, add salt; season with a little vinegar and garnish
with parsley.

Variant: In summer you can omit the cumin and add fresh green peas,
Chinese cabbage or celery.

9.38 Lettuce with fresh cheese

The bitter substances have diuretic effect and promote the blood
circulation in the digestive area. Mustard improves thyroid function,
relieves rheumatism symptoms.
Cooking time approx. 5 min
Calories p. portion: 802
1 portions
Allergens: AFM

Quantity of ingredients:
Leaf salads (bitter) 2 portions / 60g. (yes)
Fresh cheese from soya 3/8 lbs - 6oz / 150g. (yes)
Mustard 1 knife tip / 1g. (yes)
Lemon juice 1 dash / 3g. (yes)
Salt 1 pinch / 1g. (little)
Pepper (ground) 1 pinch / 0,5g. (yes)
Herbs various 2 teaspoons / 4g. (yes)
Black caraway 1 pinch / 1g. (yes)
Whole grain bread 2 slices / 40g. (recommended)

Cooking instructions:
Wash lettuce and finely pluck.
Mix 150 ml cream cheese, splashes of mustard, splashes of lemon
juice, 1 clove of garlic, chopped fresh herbs, pinch of pepper and
crushed black cumin and pour over. Serve with wholemeal bread.

9.39 Milk rice with berry juice

Laxative, strengthens kidney, strengthens eyesight, good to fight chronic constipation, strengthens kidney and bladder, diuretic, warming the body from the inside, expands blood vessels, regulates internal organs functions.
Cooking time approx. 25 min
Calories p. portion: 135
1 portions
Allergens: G

Quantity of ingredients:
Raspberry 2 table spoons / 30g. (recommended)
Cow's milk (1.5% fat) 3/4 cup - 6 oz / 200g. (yes)
Rice mash 2 table spoons / 10g. (yes)

Cooking instructions:
Thaw the frozen raspberries and then pass through a sieve. Mix half of the milk with the rice bran. Heat till it boils in a small saucepan and simmer over low heat while stirring for about 3 minutes. Remove the saucepan from the heat and gradually add the remaining milk and raspberry juice. Add the liquid to the bottle and shake vigorously. Depending on the season and preferences, add with fruit juices, glucose and from the 8th month, with honey or sugar cane granules.

9.40 Millet with pears

Refreshing and nourishing, promotes digestion, supports urination, good to fight cough, promotes perspiration, reduces blood lipids, stimulates, dissolves stagnation, forces liver, strengthens the muscles, lowers cholesterol, antiparasitic.
Cooking time approx. 35 min
Calories p. portion: 213
5 portions
Allergens: G

Quantity of ingredients:
Millet 1 cup / 120g. (yes)
Water 1 1/2 cups / 200g. (yes)
Grape juice red 1 1/2 cups / 240g. (little)
Pear 4 pieces / 600g. (yes)
Ginger fresh 1/2 teaspoon / 2g. (recommended)
Salt 1 pinch / 1g. (little)
Acerola fruit nectar or powder 1 teaspoon / 2g. (yes)

Cocoa 1 pinch / 1g. (yes)
Sunflower seeds 2 table spoons / 4g. (yes)
Barley malt 1/2 teaspoon / 2g. (yes)
Cream, sweet 30% 2 teaspoons / 20g. ()

Cooking instructions:
Simmer the millet for 5 min and let it swell for another 30 min.

Then: In a hot pot, heat some grape juice; add chopped pears, very little grated ginger, a pinch of salt, acerola, a pinch of cocoa and sauté briefly; add the boiled millet, sunflower seeds, some barley malt to taste, 1 tsp cream per serving or a little butter.

9.41 Miso soup with tofu

Vitamins, minerals and secondary plant active ingredients, invigorating, detoxifying, strengthens immune system, promotes digestion, forcing spleen, containing enzymes, reduces flatulence, alginic acid detoxifies the bowel, dissolves stagnation.
Cooking time approx. 5 min
Calories p. portion: 51
3 portions
Allergens: E

Quantity of ingredients:
Wakame 1 piece / 5g. (recommended)
Miso 3-4 table spoons / 30g. (yes)
Soy Tofu 1/8 lbs - 2oz / 50g. (yes)
Water 2 cup / 500g. (yes)
Soy sauce 1 dash / 3g. (yes)
Onion (spring onion) 1/2 teaspoon / 6g. (yes)

Cooking instructions:
Boil soybean seedlings, wakame algae and diced tofu for 5 minutes. Put the miso paste in the soup plate and slowly pour over the soup. Season with Tamari sauce. Sprinkle with cutted spring onion.

9.42 Mung bean stew

Relieves excessive thirst, supports urination, reduces blood lipids, relieves allergies. Strengthens spleen and stomach, strengthens the muscles. Lowers cholesterol, antiparasitic. Stimulates liver function, detoxifying.
Cooking time approx. 2 hours
Calories p. portion: 665
2 portions
Allergens:

Quantity of ingredients:
Mung bean 5/8 lbs - 8oz - 500g / 300g. (yes)
Sunflower oil 2 table spoons / 30g. (little)
Amaranth 1/2 teaspoon / 2g. (yes)
Fennel seeds ground 1/2 teaspoon / 2g. (yes)
Cumin (Caraway seed) 1/2 teaspoon / 2g. (recommended)
Coriander 1/2 teaspoon / 2g. (recommended)
Rice round grain 1/2 cup / 60g. (yes)
Water 3 cups / 300g. (yes)
Ginger fresh 1 inch / 3g. (recommended)
Kombu seaweed (Saccharina japonica) 1 inch / 2g. (yes)
Salt 1 pinch / 0,5g. (little)
Parsley 1 table spoon / 3g. (recommended)

Cooking instructions:
Soak mung beans overnight.
Heat sunflower oil in a hot pot. Stir in the amaranth, fennel seeds, cumin and coriander and fry briefly.
admit basmati rice, some ginger and mung beans and roast briefly.
Pour water and heat till it boils.
Add a piece of kombu alga and salt.
Simmer for 1-1/2 hours.
Garnish with parsley or coriander.

9.43 Nettle-chard soup

Nettle promotes urination, detoxifies, supporting prostate disorders, reduces inflammation, analgesic. Chard supports intestinal activity, cleans intestine.
Cooking time approx. 30 min
Calories p. portion: 52
4 portions
Allergens:

Quantity of ingredients:
Nettles Handful / 10g. (recommended)
Chard 1 lbs / 500g. (recommended)
Salt 1 pinch / 1g. (little)
Water 2 cup / 400g. (yes)
Olive oil 1 table spoon / 10g. (recommended)
Pepper (ground) 1 pinch / 0,5g. (yes)

Cooking instructions:
Heat the oil in a saucepan, add the washed and finely chopped Swiss chard. Salt and let simmer for 10 minutes. Add the chopped nettles and cook for another 10 minutes. Add pepper and puree.

9.44 Oriental rice pan

Forcing spleen, dissolves stagnation, promotes weight loss. Good to fight immunodeficiency, loss of appetite, flatulence, high blood pressure, helps to digest fat, strengthens kidney and bladder. Numerous vitamins, minerals and secondary plant active ingredients.
Cooking time approx. 30 min
Calories p. portion: 303
6 portions
Allergens: EL

Quantity of ingredients:
Rice (whole grain) 3/8 lbs - 6oz / 180g. (recommended)
Basic recipe for a vegetable soup 2 1/4 cups / 500g. (recommended)
Curry 1/2 teaspoon / 2g. (yes)
Onion (spring onion) 4 pieces / 80g. (yes)
Rapeseed oil 2 table spoons / 20g. (recommended)
Peppers 1/4 lbs - 4oz / 120g. (yes)
Corn 3 oz / 80g. (yes)
Shiitake, dried 1/2 oz / 80g. (little)
Bamboo shoots 3 oz / 80g. (yes)
Peas 3 oz / 80g. (recommended)
Peaches 1/8 lbs - 2oz / 60g. (yes)
Pineapple 1/8 lbs - 2oz / 60g. (yes)
Tomato 5/8 oz / 200g. (recommended)
Lovage 1 teaspoon / 2g. (recommended)
Basil (fresh) 1 teaspoon / 2g. (recommended)
Parsley 1 teaspoon / 2g. (recommended)
Lemon Balm (fresh) 1 teaspoon / 2g. (yes)
Pepper (ground) 1 pinch / 1g. (yes)

Cooking instructions:
Soak the mushrooms in water 20 min.
Boil the rice in the vegetable stock 15 min. and season with some curry.
Peel the onion, cut into fine cubes.
Heat the oil in a pan and sauté the onion cubes.
Wash the peppers in half, remove the core, cut into cubes and add.
Add corn, mushrooms and bamboo shoots, simmer 5 min. until firm.
Also add the bean sprouts, peas, peach cubes and pineapple cubes.
Then add the peeled, chopped tomatoes.
Add the cooked rice and season with the herbs and pepper.

9.45 Paprika-tomato rice

Good to fight little cholesterol, diabetes. Low in protein, low fat content, little protein. Forcing spleen, dissolves stagnation, promotes weight loss. Good to fight immunodeficiency, loss of appetite, flatulence, high blood pressure, depressions.
Cooking time approx. 25 min
Calories p. portion: 291
3 portions
Allergens: L

Quantity of ingredients:
Onion white 1 piece / 50g. (yes)
Peppers 4 pieces / 120g. (yes)
Bay leaf 2 pieces / 1g. (recommended)
Clove 2 pieces / 1g. (recommended)
Basic recipe for a vegetable soup 7/8 lbs / 400g. (recommended)
Rice (whole grain) 5/8 oz / 200g. (recommended)
Champignon 1/8 lbs - 2oz / 60g. (yes)
Parsley 1/2 oz / 20g. (recommended)
Pepper (ground) 1 pinch / 0,2g. (yes)
Peppers (rose peppers) 1 pinch / 0,2g. (yes)
Tomato 1/4 lbs - 4oz / 120g. (recommended)

Cooking instructions:
Finely chop the onion. Cut the peppers into fine strips.
Heat margarine in a saucepan, sauté onions and peppers, and rice.
Add the vegetable stock, add cloves and bay leaves and leave to simmer in a closed pot for approx. 20 minutes. Cut the tomato meat into 1 cm cubes and add to the rice 5 minutes before the end of cooking.

9.46 Pea dish

Supports urination, calms nerves and stomach, soothes embryo during pregnancy. Strengthens gastrointestinal function, expands blood vessels, prevents cancer, prevents diseases (in the elderly).
Cooking time approx. 1-2 hours
Calories p. portion: 406
1 portions
Allergens: CE

Quantity of ingredients:
Peas 3/8 lbs - 6oz (dried) / 150g. (recommended)
Lemon 1 piece / 40g. (yes)
Juniper berry 6 pieces / 2g. (recommended)
Sunflower oil 1 teaspoon / 3g. (little)
Pepper white (ground) 1 pinch / 0,3g. (yes)
Bay leaf 3 leaves / 2g. (recommended)
Onion white 1 piece / 50g. (yes)
Thyme 1 teaspoon / 2g. (yes)
Ginger fresh 1/2 teaspoon / 1g. (recommended)
Chicken egg 1 piece / 60g. (little)
Wakame 1 inch / 2g. (recommended)
Salt 1 pinch / 1g. (little)
Soy sauce per taste / 2g. (yes)

Cooking instructions:
Soak dried peas in plenty of cold water for several hours or overnight. Pour away soaking water and wash peas thoroughly.

Place the peas with about 1 1/2 l of cold water and heat till it boils; cook without lid for 5 minutes; scoop up the foam that forms; only then add the following ingredients: a slice of lemon, juniper berries, oil, peppercorns, bay leaves, chopped onion, dried thyme, chopped ginger, simmer about 2 strips of wakame or 1 tbsp Hijiki with lid closed for 1 - 2 hours; After 1 hour, try if the peas are already soft, because the cooking time changes with the soaking time and the age of aging; when the peas are cooked, remove the lemon slice, juniper berries and peppercorns; with salt, soy sauce, lemon juice to taste.

Note: The dish can be refrigerated for 3-4 days and heated in portions.

Serve with: crispy vegetables, rice or millet steamed in water.

9.47 Potato with dandelion salad

Promotes spleen, reduces inflammation, improves digestion, regenerates skin, supports urinating, lowers cholesterol, detoxifying, reduces inflammation, forcing spleen and digestive system, detoxifying, dissolves stagnation.
Cooking time approx. 25 min
Calories p. portion: 162
2 portions
Allergens:

Quantity of ingredients:
Potato 5/8 lbs - 8oz / 250g. (recommended)
Onion white 1/2 piece / 20g. (yes)
Sunflower oil 1 table spoon / 10g. (little)
Dandelion (young plants) 1/4 lbs - 4oz / 125g. (recommended)
Salt 1 pinch / 1g. (little)
Pepper white (ground) 1 pinch / 0,5g. (yes)

Cooking instructions:
Cook the potatoes in salted water and cut into thin slices. Finely chop the onion. Now season the potatoes with oil, salt and pepper and add the dandelion and mix.

9.48 Potato-basil soup

Reduces inflammation, improves digestion, supports urination, lowers cholesterol, reduces blood pressure, strengthens immune system, prevents cancer, reduces radiation damage, antioxidativ, dissolves stagnation.
Cooking time approx. 25 min
Calories p. portion: 96
4 portions
Allergens: L

Quantity of ingredients:
Water 2 cups / 450g. (yes)
Potato 4 pieces / 200g. (recommended)
Carrot 2 pieces / 100g. (recommended)
Celery root 1 piece / 500g. (recommended)
Pepper (ground) 1 pinch / 0,5g. (yes)
Ground 1 pinch / 1g. (yes)
Garlic 1 clove / 3g. (recommended)
Salt 1 pinch / 1g. (little)

Lemon 1 teaspoon / 3g. (yes)
Basil (fresh) 1 Bunch / 50g. (recommended)
Peppers powder 1 pinch / 1g. (yes)
Sugar cane sugar 1 pinch / 1g. (little)
Olive oil 1 table spoon / 10g. (recommended)

Cooking instructions:
Peeled and chopped 4 medium potatoes in a pot of hot water and 2
chopped medium carrots, a piece of celery root, a pinch of pepper, a
pinch of ground cumin, crushed a small clove of garlic, a pinch of salt, 1
teaspoon of lemon juice, simmer until the Vegetables is soft.

Add 1 bunch finely chopped basil into one half of the soup and puree
everything; stir in the other half of the basil; with rose paprika, a pinch of
whole cane sugar, 1 tablespoon of olive oil or butter, freshly ground
pepper, salt to taste.

9.49 Potatoes with wild garlic-curd cheese

Improves digestion, regenerates skin, supports urination, lowers
cholesterol. Helps to fight stomach pressure, belching, diabetes, acute
or chronic constipation of the intestine. Improves the flow characteristics
of the blood.
Cooking time approx. 20 min
Calories p. portion: 254
2 portions
Allergens: G

Quantity of ingredients:
Potato 3/4 lbs / 300g. (recommended)
Salt 1 pinch / 0,1g. (little)
Wild garlic (garlic spinach) 2 handful / 30g. (recommended)
Curd cheese 20% 5/8 lbs - 8oz / 250g. (recommended)
Yogurt (natural, 1.5% fat) 2 table spoons / 20g. (recommended)
Salt 1 pinch / 1g. (little)

Cooking instructions:
Cook potatoes in salted water and peel.
Wash he wild garlic leaves and carefully dried and cut into fine strips.
Mix the cottage cheese, yogurt and salt and mix in the chopped wild
garlic pieces. Serve with the potatoes.
In the season in which no wild garlic grows the wild garlic pesto can be
used.

9.50 Pumpkin curry

Promotes digestion and sweating, Dissolves stagnation, strengthens lungs and spleen, diuretic, reduces blood glucose, forcing spleen and digestive system, detoxifying, strengthens the muscles and bones.
Cooking time approx. 20 min
Calories p. portion: 193
3 portions
Allergens:

Quantity of ingredients:
Pumpkin 3/4 lbs / 300g. (recommended)
Olive oil 2 table spoons / 30g. (recommended)
Coriander 1 pinch / 1g. (recommended)
Pepper (ground) 1 pinch / 0,5g. (yes)
Curry 1 pinch / 1g. (yes)
Water 1/4 cup / 50g. (yes)
Salt 1 pinch / 1g. (little)
Parsley 1 table spoon / 7g. (recommended)
Cardamom 1 pinch / 1g. (recommended)
Turmeric (yellow root) 1 pinch / 1g. (recommended)
Rice (whole grain) 1/2 cup / 60g. (recommended)
Water 3 cups / 300g. (yes)
Salt 1 pinch / 1g. (little)

Cooking instructions:
Heat olive oil in pan. Steam the pumpkin cut in cubes, season with cilantro, pepper and curry, simmer with a little water, salt with sea salt, add chopped parsley with cardamom and turmeric, simmer on a small fire for about 10 minutes, depending on the pumpkin, the pumpkin should still be firm.
Place the rice in salted water, bring to the boil and let it simmer over low heat for about 15 minutes.

9.51 Pumpkin soup

Promotes digestion, forcing spleen and stomach, reduces blood pressure, strengthens immune system, prevents cancer, reduces radiation damage, improves digestion, regenerates skin, lowers cholesterol, reduces blood glucose, protects liver.
Cooking time approx. 1 hour
Calories p. portion: 105
3 portions
Allergens:

Quantity of ingredients:
Pumpkin 3/4 lbs / 300g. (recommended)
Carrot 2 pieces / 100g. (recommended)
Potato 2 pieces / 120g. (recommended)
Olive oil 1 table spoon / 10g. (recommended)
Onion white 1 piece / 50g. (yes)
Water 1 cup / 120g. (yes)
Parsley 1 table spoon / 7g. (recommended)
Anise (Common Fennel) 1 pinch / 1g. (recommended)
Salt 1 pinch / 1g. (little)

Cooking instructions:
Add the olive oil to the pan, add the diced pumpkin, diced carrots and potatoes. Roast them shortly, add the finely chopped onion, fill with water, add enough water to cover the vegetables at least 3 finger-widths. Boil at low heat.

Season with sea salt, add small cutted parsley, a pinch of anise (little).

Allow to simmer for about 35 minutes. Then purée the soup and add some water, depending on the consistency of the soup.

9.52 Pumpkin-yoghurt soup

Relaxes, reduces blood pressure, strengthens immune system, promotes weight loss. Good to fight immunodeficiency, loss of appetite, flatulence, depressions, diabetes, diarrhea.
Cooking time approx. 15 min
Calories p. portion: 68
4 portions
Allergens: GL

Quantity of ingredients:
Basic recipe for a vegetable soup 1 cup / 300g. (recommended)
Hokkaido pumpkin 1,1 lbs / 500g. (recommended)
Ginger fresh 1/2 teaspoon / 2g. (recommended)
Fennel seeds ground 1/2 teaspoon / 1g. (yes)
Anise (Common Fennel) 1/4 teaspoon / 1g. (recommended)
Yogurt (natural, 1.5% fat) 3/8 lbs - 6oz / 150g. (recommended)
Peppermint 2 leaves / 1g. (recommended)
Salt 1 pinch / 1g. (little)

Cooking instructions:
Heat the vegetable broth (after the basic recipe) till it boils . Add diced pumpkin, chopped ginger, crushed fennel seeds and anise. Bring the soup to the boil and simmer for about 12 minutes until the pumpkin is soft.
Remove soup from the heat. Puree the soup with the yoghurt with the blender. Serve soup with finely chopped mint sprinkled.

9.53 Quick zucchini soup

Diuretic, supports urination. Strengthens gastrointestinal function, expands blood vessels, prevents cancer, prevents diseases (in the elderly). Stimulates liver function, detoxifying.
Cooking time approx. 10 min
Calories p. portion: 42
4 portions
Allergens:

Quantity of ingredients:
Zucchini 2-3 pieces / 500g. (recommended)
Onion white 1 piece / 50g. (yes)
Corn germ oil 2 table spoons / 6g. (little)
Parsley 1 table spoon / 7g. (recommended)
Chives 1 teaspoon / 3g. (recommended)
Water 2 cup / 400g. (yes)

Cooking instructions:
Fry chopped onion in oil. Add sliced zucchini and sauté well. Pour with water. Chop parsley and chives, add and puree everything.

9.54 Quinoa piquant with avocado

Anti-inflammatory, good to fight swelling, pain and itching. Reduces blood pressure, strengthens immune system. Strengthens gastrointestinal function, expands blood vessels. Good to fight gastrointestinal complaints.
Cooking time approx. 20 min
Calories p. portion: 561
2 portions
Allergens:

Quantity of ingredients:
Water 1 1/2 cups / 240g. (yes)
Quinoa 1 cup / 100g. (yes)
Carrot 1 piece shredded / 100g. (recommended)
Onion (spring onion) 2 table spoons (chopped) / 12g. (yes)
Curcuma 1/2 teaspoon / 1g. (yes)
Avocado 1 piece soft / 300g. (yes)
Salt 1 pinch / 0,5g. (little)
Pepper (ground) 1 pinch / 0,2g. (yes)
Linseed oil 2 teaspoons / 4g. (yes)

Cooking instructions:
Put quinoa in hot water.
Add grated carrot, pepper and salt, finely chopped spring onion and turmeric.
Simmer about 20 minutes, pull from the fire.
Add pre-cut avocado.
Add a dash of oil and sprinkle with fresh parsley and gomasio.

Spices and herbs: turmeric, cardamom, cress, parsley, chives.

Variation: For those who want more hearty, you can also use a sardine from organic fish preserves. If you are the "protein type", this breakfast will hold on for a long time!

9.55 Refreshing cucumber soup with potatoes

Diuretic, detoxifying, suppresses conversion of sugar into fat, lowers cholesterol, prevents cancer, reduces inflammation, improves digestion, lowers cholesterol, dissolves stagnation, improves blood circulation, stimulates appetite.
Cooking time approx. 15 min
Calories p. portion: 148
3 portions
Allergens: GN

Quantity of ingredients:
Sesame oil 1 table spoon / 10g. (little)
Potato 4 pieces / 300g. (recommended)
Onion (spring onion) 3 pieces / 60g. (yes)
Pepper (ground) 1 pinch / 0,5g. (yes)
Nutmeg 1 pinch / 1g. (recommended)
Salt 1 pinch / 1g. (little)

Lemon 1/2 piece / 25g. (yes)
Cucumber 2 pieces / 500g. (yes)
Cream, sweet 30% 1 table spoon / 10g. ()
Dill 1 table spoon / 15g. (recommended)

Cooking instructions:
Sauté sesame oil, chopped potatoes, plenty of spring onions in a hot pot; add pepper, a little nutmeg, salt, lemon juice, hot water, diced cucumber; simmer for about 10 minutes and then puree; add some sweet cream as you like, fresh dill.

Variation: Add a little chili, oregano, thyme or rosemary to soften the cooling effect.

9.56 Rice noodle soup with shiitake mushrooms

Very light and powerful. Strengthens the immune system.
Cooking time approx. 20 min
Calories p. portion: 66
2 portions
Allergens: L

Quantity of ingredients:
Rice noodles 2 handful / 20g. (yes)
Shiitake, dried 4-6 pieces / 5g. (little)
Basic recipe for a vegetable soup (nutritious) 1 1/2 cups / 240g. (recommended)
Chinese cabbage 1 cup / 60g. (recommended)
Lovage 1 teaspoon / 3g. (recommended)
Miso 2 table spoons / 18g. (yes)

Cooking instructions:
Soak rice noodles and shiitake mushrooms separately in cold water. Heat the vegetable broth and add the soaked shiitake mushrooms cut into strips and simmer gently. Cut Chinese cabbage into noodles, add lovage green and rice noodles and let it steep for a while. Before serving, stir in Miso dissolved in a little cooled water.

Recommendation: Suitable at the beginning of each meal, also for breakfast

9.57 Rice with stewed vegetables

Reduces blood pressure, strengthens immune system, prevents cancer, reduces radiation damage, extremely low fat content, good to fight blood circulation disorders, thrombose, risk of embolism, a headache, heart attack and stroke. Is diuretic.
Cooking time approx. 20 min
Calories p. portion: 166
2 portions
Allergens: L

Quantity of ingredients:
Rice variety any 1/2 cup / 60g. (yes)
Water 3 cups / 300g. (yes)
Lemon peel 1 piece / 3g. (yes)
Water 1/2 cup / 0g. (yes)
Carrot 2 pieces / 180g. (recommended)
Celery sticks 1/2 piece / 5g. (recommended)
Champignon 1/2 cup / 50g. (yes)
Cress 2 table spoons / 20g. (recommended)
Linseed oil 1 dash / 3g. (yes)

Cooking instructions:
Cook rice according to basic recipe with a piece of lemon peel.
Steam chopped carrots, celery and mushrooms until soft.
Then sprinkle with cress. Then add a dash of high quality cold oil.

9.58 Roasted barley patties

Improves digestion, lowers cholesterol, good to fight diarrhea, ulceration, joint pain, stomach problems. Promotes spleen and liver, reduces blood pressure, strengthens immune system, prevents cancer, reduces radiation damage, stimulates liver function.
Cooking time approx. 1 1/2 hours
Calories p. portion: 398
3 portions
Allergens: ACN

Quantity of ingredients:
Water 1 1/2 cups / 250g. (yes)
Barley grouts 1 cup / 120g. (yes)
Potato 1 piece / 140g. (recommended)
Carrot 1 piece / 120g. (recommended)
Champignon 2-3 pieces / 25g. (yes)

Chicken egg 1 piece / 55g. (little)
Onion white 1 piece / 50g. (yes)
Ginger fresh 1/2 teaspoon / 1g. (recommended)
Pepper (ground) 1 pinch / 0,5g. (yes)
Salt 1 pinch / 1g. (little)
Lemon 1/2 piece / 15g. (yes)
Parsley 2 table spoons / 15g. (recommended)
Peppers powder 1 pinch / 1g. (yes)
Sesame oil 2 table spoons / 50g. (little)
Bread roll 1 piece / 35g. (little)

Cooking instructions:
Preparation:
Place 2 large cups of hot water in a saucepan; add 1 large cup of barley porridge; simmer for 2 minutes while stirring; then let it swell for 20 minutes on the switched off stove; take down and let cool.

Cook in boiling water 1 large potato, chopped and cut.

Soak 1 roll in hot water and squeeze well.

Then: Mix the barley groats and crushed the potato. Add 1 grated carrot, 2 - 3 chopped mushrooms, 1 egg, 1 finely chopped onion, 1/2 teaspoon grated ginger, a pinch of pepper, a pinch of salt, a little lemon juice, chopped parsley, plenty of rose paprika; knead well and form patties; heat sesame oil in a hot pan; fry the patties for about 15 minutes over a gentle heat; turn at half time.

Also fits well: lettuce, soybean vegetables.

9.59 Roasted millet with Celery sticks

Promotes spleen and kidney, diuretic, promoting metabolism.
Cooking time approx. 30 min
Calories p. portion: 400
2 portions
Allergens: L

Quantity of ingredients:
Millet 1 cup / 120g. (yes)
Water 1 1/2 cups / 240g. (yes)
Celery sticks 2 rods / 50g. (recommended)
Water 2 table spoons / 30g. (yes)

Herbs various 1 table spoon / 10g. (yes)
Salt 1 pinch / 1g. (little)
Sage 3-4 leaves / 2g. (recommended)
Cress 1 teaspoon / 3g. (recommended)

Cooking instructions:
Roast millet briefly, pour over water, heat till it boils and let stand for 20 min. to swell.

Cut celery into small pieces and mix with water, salt and fresh herbs and cook for 10 min. Add to the millet.
Sprinkle fresh sage or watercress over it.

9.60 Rosemary Potatoes

Reduces Inflammation, improves digestion, regenerates skin, supports urination, lowers cholesterol. Rosemary stimulates digestion, strengthens lung, promotes spleen and kidney, dries out.
Cooking time approx. 30 min
Calories p. portion: 188
2 portions
Allergens:

Quantity of ingredients:
Potato 6-8 pieces / 420g. (recommended)
Salt (herbal) 1 pinch / 1g. (little)
Olive oil 1 table spoon / 10g. (recommended)
Rosemary 1 teaspoon / 2g. (yes)

Cooking instructions:
Cut the potatoes into half´s, apply a little olive oil on the cut surface, then salt, sprinkle 2 - 3 rosemary needles on the potatoes.
Place the potatoes on the baking tray and bake them in the preheated oven for approx. 25 minutes to 190°C/374°F.

9.61 Rucola salad with tomatoes

Promotes digestion, helps to digest fat, supports urination, reduces blood pressure, stimulates digestion, strengthens the muscles, antioxidativ, helps to fight gastritis, flatulence and heartburn.
Cooking time approx. 10 min
Calories p. portion: 129
1 portions
Allergens: O

Quantity of ingredients:
Olive oil 1 table spoon / 10g. (recommended)
Pepper (ground) 1 pinch / 0,2g. (yes)
Salt 1 pinch / 0,3g. (little)
Vinegar (Apple vinegar) 1 dash / 1g. (recommended)
Tomato 4 pieces / 200g. (recommended)
Rucola 2 handful / 30g. (recommended)

Cooking instructions:
In a salad bowl stir in olive oil, freshly ground pepper, salt, vinegar and diced tomatoes; plenty of finely shredded rucola leaves.
Variants: Cut shiitake mushrooms into fine strips: Fry one half in a little butter and mix with the other half of raw shiitake under the salad. In place of shiitake mushrooms can be used.
Serve with: toasted bread, polenta.

9.62 Semolina mash with grape puree

Protects the digestive system. Affects anorexia, good to fight flatulence, inflammatory bowel disease. Strengthens tendons and bones, supports urination, promotes digestion. Little laxative.
Cooking time approx. 10 min
Calories p. portion: 204
1 portions
Allergens: AG

Quantity of ingredients:
Grapes white 6 pieces / 15g. (recommended)
Cow's milk (1.5% fat) 3/4 cup - 6 oz / 200g. (yes)
Wheat semolina for children 2 table spoons / 30g. (yes)

Cooking instructions:
Wash the grapes, cut in half, remove the peel and remove the seeds. Finely chop the pulp, collecting the juice. Heat half of the milk. Add the semolina (not whole wheat), heat till it boils and simmer over low heat with stirring in about 3 minutes. Remove the pot from the cooking area and gradually add the remaining milk and the grape marc.
You can easily sweeten semolina pudding with fruit purée or fruit juice.

9.63 Semolina soup with vegetables

Reduces blood pressure, strengthens immune system, prevents cancer, forcing spleen, dissolves stagnation, promotes weight loss. Good to fight immunodeficiency, loss of appetite, flatulence, high blood pressure, depressions, diabetes, diarrhea, rheumatism, heartburn, twelffinger intestinal ulcers.
Cooking time approx. 20 min
Calories p. portion: 105
3 portions
Allergens: AGL

Quantity of ingredients:
Basic recipe for a vegetable soup 2 cup / 500g. (recommended)
Wheat semolina 2 table spoons / 20g. (yes)
Lovage 1/2 teaspoon / 2g. (recommended)
Basil (fresh) 1/2 teaspoon / 1g. (recommended)
Nutmeg 1 pinch / 0,1g. (recommended)
Carrot 1/4 lbs - 4oz / 100g. (recommended)
Celery root 1/8 lbs - 2oz / 50g. (recommended)
Cream, sweet 30% 2 table spoons / 30g. ()
Parsley 1 table spoon / 10g. (recommended)

Cooking instructions:
Roast wheat grits without fat in a pan. Roast the chopped carrots and celery briefly. Add the vegetable soup (Basic recipe for a vegetable soup). Season with lovage, nutmeg and let it 10 min. simmer.
Stir in the cream before serving and garnish with parsley.

9.64 Spelled with fruit and nuts

Stops diarrhea, promotes digestion, appetizing, relieves fatigue, anti-inflammatory (gastrointestinal). Good to fight tumor lesions and leukemia, is antiallergic in food allergies, regulates metabolism, lowers blood glucose and cholesterol.
Cooking time approx. 1 1/2 hours
Calories p. portion: 290
3 portions
Allergens: AH

Quantity of ingredients:
Spelled grain 1 cup / 120g. (yes)
Water 1 cup / 50g. (yes)
Apple (sweet) 1 piece / 220g. (recommended)
Apricot 1 piece / 200g. (yes)
Peaches 1 piece / 120g. (yes)
Cinnamon ground 1 pinch / 1g. (recommended)
Cardamom 1 pinch / 1g. (recommended)
Salt 1 pinch / 1g. (little)
Strawberries 1 cup / 120g. (recommended)
Almond puree 1 table spoon / 15g. (little)
Cocoa 1 pinch / 1g. (yes)
Walnuts 1 table spoon / 10g. (yes)

Cooking instructions:
Put spelled in hot water and cook.

Then: Give sweet chopped fruit (apples, apricots, peaches) in a little hot water, with a little cinnamon, sauté briefly; ground cardamom and / or coriander, a small pinch of salt, the boiled spelled, berries after season. Put some cocoa and roasted nuts over it.

9.65 Spicy avocado cream with cottage cheese

Anti-inflammatory, good to fight swelling, pain and itching, forcing spleen and digestive system, detoxifying, bactericide.
Cooking time approx. 15 min
Calories p. portion: 614
4 portions
Allergens: G

Quantity of ingredients:
Avocado 2 pieces / 600g. (yes)
Pepper (ground) 1 pinch / 0,5g. (yes)
Salt 1 pinch / 1g. (little)
Lemon juice 1/2 piece / 15g. (yes)
Peppers powder 1 pinch / 1g. (yes)
Olive oil 1 table spoon / 10g. (recommended)
Herbs various 1 table spoon / 7g. (yes)
Cottage cheese 1 cup / 250g. (recommended)
Bread with carob kernel flour 8 slices / 200g. (yes)

Cooking instructions:
Peel, core and purée avocados; add plenty of ground pepper, salt, lemon juice, rose paprika, a few drops of oil, chili, fresh chopped herbs, a pinch of salt; cottage cheese (about the same amount as avocado cream), carefully submerge.

Goes well with: Potatoes and millet, with which the avocado cream in combination with vegetable dishes, legumes or lettuce leaves a delicious meal. It is also very good as an appetizer, as a souvenir at parties and as a morning meal in the summer together with a mild dish of lentils or Adzuki beans and grated radish.

9.66 Tea from cinnamon sticks

Antibacterial, good to fight vomiting, loss of appetite, flatulence, diabetes. Improves blood circulation, antipyretic, diuretic, cramp-dissolving, mucus-releasing, analgesic, diaphoretic, reduces the blood glucose level.
Cooking time approx. 15 min
Calories p. portion: 2
1 portions
Allergens:

Quantity of ingredients:
Cinnamon sticks 1/4 piece / 1g. (recommended)
Water 1 cup / 125g. (yes)

Cooking instructions:
A quarter of a cinnamon stick for a cup of tea. Start cold and bring to the boil. Let it sit for 15 minutes, then strain.
This tea is unsweetened and swallowed, slowly drunk. The amount is enough for one day.

9.67 Tea Green tea

Green tea promotes digestion, supports urination, dissolves mucus, detoxifying, stimulates nerves, reduces blood lipids, lowers cholesterol, reduces inflammation.
Cooking time approx. 10 min
Calories p. portion: 2
1 portions
Allergens:

Quantity of ingredients:
Green tea 1 teaspoon / 2g. (recommended)
Water 1 cup / 120g. (yes)

Cooking instructions:
For each cup you use a teaspoonful or a teabag.
Pour green tea only with 60 to 80 ° C / 140 to 176 °F hot water, otherwise it will be bitter.
If the tea has a stimulating effect, let it draw for two to three minutes. It has a calming effect for a duration of five minutes (no longer, otherwise it will be bitter!).
Another method: Pour the tea leaves with about 70 ° C / 158 °F hot water and pour the water immediately again.
Then just pour hot water again. The bitter substances disappear and the tea gets a milder aroma.

9.68 Thick pea soup

Supports urination, detoxifying, dissolves stagnation, improves blood circulation, strengthens liver and kidney, strengthens immune system.
Cooking time approx. 2-3 hours
Calories p. portion: 123
3 portions
Allergens: AN

Quantity of ingredients:
Peas, green 3/8 lbs - 6oz / 150g. (recommended)
Water 2 1/4 cups / 550g. (yes)
Sesame oil 1 table spoon / 20g. (little)
Onion white 1/2 piece / 25g. (yes)
Ginger fresh 1/2 teaspoon / 1g. (recommended)
Ground 1/2 teaspoon / 1g. (yes)
Oat meal 1 table spoon / 15g. (yes)
Salt 1 pinch / 1g. (little)
Parsley 1 stem / 2g. (recommended)

Cooking instructions:
Soak dried peas before cooking. Sauté sesame oil, onion, a little oatmeal, ginger and cumin in a hot pot; add the peas and simmer for 2-3 hours; add salt at the end and purée with a blender; garnish with parsley.

9.69 Vegetable bowl with tofu and curry on rice

Diuretic, reduces blood glucose. Reduces flatulence, supports digestion. Contains ideal herbal mucus, which provides regeneration of the small and large intestinal flora. Reduces blood pressure.
Cooking time approx. 30 min
Calories p. portion: 162
6 portions
Allergens: E

Quantity of ingredients:
Olive oil 2 table spoons / 20g. (recommended)
Garlic 2 cloves / 3g. (recommended)
Onion white 1 piece / 60g. (yes)
Curry 2 table spoons / 16g. (yes)
Water 2 cup / 500g. (yes)
Turnips 2 pieces / 50g. (recommended)
Pumpkin 1 piece / 400g. (recommended)
Carrot 1 piece / 100g. (recommended)
Parsnip 1 piece / 150g. (recommended)
Potato 1 piece / 70g. (recommended)
Sweet potato 1 piece / 70g. (yes)
Cauliflower 1/4 piece / 250g. (yes)
Broccoli 1/2 piece / 250g. (recommended)
Okra 12 pieces / 200g. (yes)
Soy Tofu 1 piece / 250g. (yes)
Basil 2 table spoons / 12g. (yes)
Salt 1 pinch / 0,5g. (little)

Cooking instructions:
Heat the oil at medium temperature in a large, heavy casserole, add the garlic and onion and sauté with constant stirring. Sprinkle curry powder over it, fry gently for about 5 minutes and make sure that the garlic and curry do not burn. Add the water and heat till it boils. Gradually peel all vegetables, dice and add, starting with the varieties that need the longest cooking time. Once the water has boiled again, reduce the heat and simmer the vegetables for about 15 minutes. When it is almost soft. Add the cauliflower and broccoli florets and the okra and cook the stew for another 10 to 15 minutes. Add the tofu during the last 5 minutes. Cook the brown rice at the same time: Sprinkle the rice in a medium saucepan with water, salt and cover for about 20 minutes. cook on a low heat. Take from the fire and another 10 min. to let go.
Arrange the stew over the brown rice and sprinkle with basil.

9.70 Vegetable rice

Forcing spleen, dissolves stagnation, promotes weight loss. Good to fight immunodeficiency, loss of appetite, flatulence, high blood pressure, strengthens kidney and bladder. Diuretic, warming the body from the inside, regulates internal organs functions.
Cooking time approx. 30 min
Calories p. portion: 304
3 portions
Allergens: L

Quantity of ingredients:
Broccoli 1/8 lbs - 2oz / 50g. (recommended)
Carrot 1/8 lbs - 2oz / 50g. (recommended)
Kohlrabi 1/8 lbs - 2oz / 50g. (yes)
Cauliflower 1 oz / 30g. (yes)
Peas 1/2 oz / 20g. (recommended)
Margarine 1 teaspoon / 4g. (little)
Rice (whole grain) 5/8 oz / 200g. (recommended)
Basic recipe for a vegetable soup (nutritious) 7/8 lbs / 400g. (recommended)
Parsley 1/2 oz / 20g. (recommended)
Pepper (ground) 1 pinch / 0,2g. (yes)

Cooking instructions:
Cut the broccoli, carrots and kohlrabi into small cubes, divide the cauliflower into small florets. Heat the margarine in a pan or saucepan, sauté the vegetables. Then add the rice, top up with the vegetable stock and leave to soak for 15-20 minutes.

In the meantime finely chop the parsley. After cooking, season the rice with freshly ground pepper and parsley.

9.71 Vegetable semolina soup

Diuretic, harmonizes the stomach and intestines, conducts bowel winds, reduces blood pressure, lowers cholesterol, detoxifying, good to fight loss of appetite, flatulence, inflammatory bowel disease, heartburn, twelffinger intestinal ulcers. Stimulates digestion, reduces pain.
Cooking time approx. 20 min
Calories p. portion: 199
3 portions
Allergens: AEGL

Quantity of ingredients:
Basic recipe for a vegetable soup 2 cup / 500g. (recommended)
Potato 1 piece / 80g. (recommended)
Parsnip 1 piece / 180g. (recommended)
Carrot 1 piece / 120g. (recommended)
Celery root 3/8 lbs - 6oz / 150g. (recommended)
Kohlrabi 1/2 piece / 200g. (yes)
Beans (green, fresh) 1/4 lbs / 100g. (recommended)
Wheat semolina 2 table spoons / 24g. (yes)
Lovage 1/2 teaspoon / 2g. (recommended)
Butter organic 1 table spoon / 20g. ()
Soy sauce 1 teaspoon / 3g. (yes)

Cooking instructions:
Worm the prepared vegetable soup; cook the vegetables in the soup softly. Spread some wheatgrass and let it swell. At the end, add lovage-green and a little butter and taste with soy sauce.

9.72 Wild garlic cream soup

Reduces blood pressure, strengthens immune system, good to fight acute or chronic constipation. Improves the flow characteristics of the blood.
Cooking time approx. 15 min
Calories p. portion: 232
4 portions
Allergens: GL

Quantity of ingredients:
Wild garlic (garlic spinach) 5/8 lbs - 8oz / 250g. (recommended)
Onion (spring onion) 2 pieces / 40g. (yes)
Basic recipe for a vegetable soup 3 cups / 750g. (recommended)
Cream (30% fat) 5/8 lbs - 8oz / 250g. ()
Salt 1 pinch / 1g. (little)

Cooking instructions:
Wash the wild garlic leaves and dry them carefully. Cut the wild garlic leaves into fine strips. (Dried wild garlic: Leave approx. 80g in 40g of water for 10 minutes.)
Shortly fry the wild garlic with the finely diced onion in hot butter, deglaze with the vegetable stock and simmer over medium heat for 10 minutes. Then puree the soup, refine with whipped cream and season with salt.

9.73 Wild garlic dumplings

Improves the flow characteristics of the blood, reduces blood pressure, lowers cholesterol.
Cooking time approx. 30 min
Calories p. portion: 906
4 portions
Allergens: ACG

Quantity of ingredients:
Potato (mealy) 1,1 lbs / 500g. (recommended)
Wild garlic (garlic spinach) 5/8 oz / 200g. (recommended)
Butter (half fat) 1/8 lbs - 2oz / 40g. ()
Wheat flour 3/8 lbs - 6oz / 150g. (little)
Wheat semolina 1/8 lbs - 2oz / 50g. (yes)
Chicken yolk 2 pieces / 20g. (little)
Onion white 1 piece / 50g. (yes)
Butter (half fat) 1/2 oz / 10g. ()
Tomato 5/8 oz / 200g. (recommended)
Sugar white 1 pinch / 1g. (little)
Turkey ham 5/8 lbs - 8oz / 250g. (little)
Olive oil 1 table spoon / 10g. (recommended)
Parmesan 1/8 lbs - 2oz / 50g. ()
Salt 1 pinch / 1g. (little)
Pepper (ground) 1 pinch / 0,5g. (yes)
Nutmeg 1 pinch / 0,5g. (recommended)

Cooking instructions:
Boil potatoes in salted water, peel and squeeze through the press while still hot.
Fresh wild garlic: wash, clean and briefly dive into sparkling boiling salt water (blanch). Quench cold and express.
Coarsely chop the wild garlic.
Dried wild garlic: Leave approx. 100g wild garlic in 100g of water for 10 minutes and use with the water.

Melt 50g of the butter. Mix flour, semolina, egg yolks and liquid butter with the potato mixture, knead in wild garlic.
Season with salt and pepper and grated nutmeg and let rest for about 15 minutes.

Peel onion, finely chop and fry in the remaining butter. Add chopped tomatoes, simmer for a few minutes, season with salt and pepper and sugar.

Make 3 dumplings per person from the potato mixture. Soak in salted water for about 15 minutes.

In the meantime lightly fry the ham in oil. Rub the cheese. Drain the dumplings, serve with the ham, the tomato sauce and grated cheese.

9.74 Yellow lentil soup

Strengthens heart and kidney, diuretic, promotes spleen, calms the stomach, promotes digestion, strengthens immune system, prevents cancer, reduces radiation damage, stimulates liver function, antioxidativ.
Cooking time approx. 20 min
Calories p. portion: 155
7 portions
Allergens: A

Quantity of ingredients:
Lentils yellow 1 lbs / 500g. (yes)
Carrot 2 pieces / 150g. (recommended)
Kohlrabi 1 piece / 300g. (yes)
Onion white 1 piece / 50g. (yes)
Parsley 1/2 bunch / 100g. (recommended)
Turmeric (yellow root) 1 pinch / 1g. (recommended)
Cardamom 1 pinch / 1g. (recommended)
Salt 1 pinch / 1g. (little)
Olive oil 1 table spoon / 10g. (recommended)
Water 4 cup / 1000g. (yes)
Lemon juice 1/2 piece / 15g. (yes)
White bread (wheat bread) 7 slices / 140g. (little)

Cooking instructions:
Wash lenses well in a colander. Heat oil in a pot. Add finely chopped onion, sliced carrots, diced kohlrabi and spices, sauté and salt. Add the lentils and cover with water and simmer for 20 minutes. Add water as needed and season with salt. Sprinkle with fresh parsley or fresh green cilantro and drizzle with lemon juice.
Here you can also use red lenses. (same cooking time).
Serve with white bread.

10 Effects of food

10.1 Use ingredients: recommendable

Acai powder
Anchovy / Sardine
Angelica root
Anise (Common Fennel)
Apple (sour)
Apple (sweet)
Apple puree
Artichoke
Asparagus (green or white)
Aubergine
Banchatee (green tea)
barberry
Basic recipe for a vegetable soup (nutritious)
Basil (fresh)
Bay leaf
Beans (green, fresh)
Bearberry leaf
Bitter Herb liqueur
Bitter liqueur
Blackberry dried (unripe fruit)
Blackberry´s
Blueberry
Borage
Borage oil
Broccoli
Buttermilk
Cardamom
Carrot
Carrot (Early Carrot)
Carrot juice without sugar
Celery root
Celery sticks
Chamomile tea
Chard
Chervil dried
Chicory
Chinese cabbage
Chives
Chrysanthemum blossom tea
Cinnamon ground
Cinnamon sticks
Clove
Coriander
Cottage cheese
Cranberry
Cranberry juice
Cream 10% coffee cream
Cress

Cucumber (bitter)
Cumin (Caraway seed)
Curd cheese 20%
Currant (black)
Currant (red)
Currant (white)
Dandelion (young plants)
Dill
Dyer's broom herb
Elderberries
Elderberry blossom tee
Endive salad
Fennel
Flower pollen
Fox nut, gorgon nut, makhana
Garlic
Ginger fresh
Goat and sheep's blood
Goat and sheep's brain
Goat and sheep's stomach
Gooseberry
Gourd
Grapes red
Grapes white
Green spelt
Green tea
Ground caraway
Herbal tea mix
Herring
Hibiscus
Hokkaido pumpkin
Hyssop
Juniper berry
King Solomon's-seal
Kudzu
Kumquats
Lamb's lettuce
Lamb's lettuce
Lily bulbs
Linseed
Lovage
Mackerel
Mascarpone cheese
Mung bean sprouting
Nettles
Nori, purple seaweed, red algae
Nutmeg
Olive oil
Orange blossom

Orange dried peel
Orange grated peel
Oregano dried
Oregano fresh
Parsley
Parsnip
Peas
Peas, green
Peppermint
Peppermint tea
Peppers (sweet)
Potato
Potato (mealy)
Pumpkin
Quince
Radicchio
Radish
Radish (white, green, purple-red)
Radish horseradish
Rapeseed oil
Raspberry
Raspberry dried (immature)
Red beet
Rhubarb
Rice (whole grain)
Rose hip
Rose hip tea
Rucola
Sage
Salmon
Salsify
Savory
Sour milk

Sour milk cheese 20%
St. Benedict's thistle, blessed thistle,
holy thistle, spotted thistle
Strawberries
Thyme dried
Tomato
Tomato juice
Tomato paste
Tomato puree
Tuna
Turmeric (yellow root)
Turnip
Turnips
Vegetable juice
Vinegar (Apple vinegar)
Vinegar Aceto Balsamico
Wakame
Walnut oil
Water hot
Watermelon
Wax gourd
Wheat germ oil
Whey
Whole grain bread
Wholemeal flour
Wild garlic (garlic spinach)
Wild herbs
Yarrow
Yarrow tea
Yew nut
Yogurt (natural, 1.5% fat)
Zucchini

10.2 Use ingredients: yes

Acerola fruit nectar or powder
Adzuki beans
Agar agar (kelp)
Agave nectar
Agrimony
Almond
Aloe juice
Amaranth
Amaranth Pops
Apple juice (natural cloudy)
Apricot
Apricots
Arrowroot
Avocado
Baking powder
Balm
Bamboo shoots
Banana

Banana (cooking banana)
Barley
Barley flour
Barley grass powder
Barley grouts
Barley malt
Barley not peeled
Basic recipe for a fish soup
Basic recipe for a rice soup (Congee)
Basil
Batavia
Berries of the season
Berry juice
Bitter Lemon
Bitter orange peel
Black beans
Black caraway
Black fungus mushroom

Black tea
Blackberry leaves
Black-eyed peas
Blackthorn (Sloe)
Blue mallow tee
Blueberry dried
Bocksdorn fruits (Fructus Lycii, Goji, goji berry dried
Boletus mushroom
Boxhorn clover seeds
Brazil nuts
Bread with carob kernel flour
Broad beans (thick beans)
Brussels sprouts
Buckbean
Buckwheat
Buckwheat (roasted) Kasha
Buckwheat whole grain
Bulgur (cereals)
Burdock root tea
Bush beans
Butter beans white
Cantaloupe
Capers in olive oil
Carambola (Star fruit)
Carob flour, St. john's bread
Cashews
Cauliflower
Cereal coffee
Chamomile
Champignon
Channa-Dal
Chanterelle
Chenpi (chinese tangerine bowl)
Cherry
Cherry (sour)
Cherry compote
Chervil
Chicken egg white
Chickpeas
Chili (pod or ground)
Chinese pearl barley
Chlorella (fresh water)
Clementine
Clementines
Cocoa
Coconut flakes
Coconut grated
Coconut meat
Coconut milk
Cod
Codfish
Coffee
Coix (seeds) YiYi Ren

Compote (fruits of the season)
Coriander (fresh)
Corn
Corn (fast polenta)
Corn (roasted)
Corn flour
Corn Grease (Polenta)
Corn silk tea
Corn starch
Couscous
Cow's milk (1.5% fat)
Cranberries
Cranberry
Cream sour 10%
Creamer
Crispbread
Crucian
Cucumber
Cucumber (spicy cucumber)
Curcuma
Curry
Curry paste red
Daisy
Dandelion juice
Dandelionroots tea
Dashi
Dulse (seaweed)
Fennel seeds ground
Fennel tea
Fenugreek (Trigonella foenum-graecum)
Fig
Fish pieces mixed (fresh water)
Flounder
French beans
Fresh cheese from soya
Freshwater fish
Fruit tea
Gail plum
Galangal
Garam Masala powder
Gelatin white
Gelee Royal
Gentian root
Gentian root tea
Ginger powder
Ginkgo fruit
Ginseng
Ginseng root
Goat and sheep's milk
Goat cheese
Grapefruit (Pomelo)
Grapefruit dried peel
Grapefruit juice

Grapeseed oil
Ground
Guava
Halibut (Flatfish)
Hawthorn
Hazelnuts
Herbs bitter
Herbs of Provence
Herbs various
Herbs wild
Hibiscus tea
Hijiki
Hop
Horehound leaves
Iceberg lettuce
Jasmine blossoms tee
Kaki plum
Kalmus
Kefir
Kidney beans (red)
Kiwi
Kohlrabi
Kombu seaweed (Saccharina japonica)
Kukicha tea
Lavender blossoms
Leaf salads (bitter)
Leek
Lemon
Lemon Balm (dried)
Lemon Balm (fresh)
Lemon juice
Lemon peel
Lemongrass
Lentils
Lentils black
Lentils red
Lentils yellow
Lettuce
Licorice root tea
Lima beans
Lime
Lime blossom tea
Linseed (crushed)
Linseed oil
Liver smoothing tea
Loquate / Japanese medlar
Lotus roots
Lotus seeds
Lovage seeds
Luo Han Guo fruit
Lychee
Lychee in Preserved
Lye roll
Mallow (Malva sylvestris) blossom tea

Malt
Mango
Manioc flour
Mare's milk
Marjoram
Mediterranean fish (cod, plaice, haddock, sea eel, mackerel)
Medlar
Millet
Millet flakes
Mineral water
Mirabelle plum
Miso
Miso black (fermented)
Miso paste (soy bean paste)
Mixed Pickles
Mu Erh Mushroom
Muesli
Mulberry fruit
Mulled Wine Spice
Mullet
Multi-grain bread (gray bread)
Mung bean
Mustard
Mustard Dijon
Mustard medium hot
Mustard seeds
Mustard sweet
Mutton
Nasturtium (nose-twister or nose-tweaker)
Nectarine
Noodles (whole grain) with egg
Oat
Oat flakes (whole grain)
Oat flakes roasted
Oat flour
Oat fusion (baby food)
Oat meal
Oat milk
Okra
Olives
Olives green
Onion (shallot)
Onion (spring onion)
Onion read
Onion white
Orange
Orange peel
Papaya
Parsley root
Passion blossoms tea
Passion fruit
Peaches

Peaches (canned)
Pear
Pearl barley
Pearl barley
Pepper (ground)
Pepper Cayenne
Pepper powder (hot)
Pepper white (ground)
Peppercorns
Pepperoni
Pepperoni, red, pitted, halved
Pepperoni, yellow, pitted, halved
Peppers
Peppers (rose peppers)
Peppers powder
Perch
Pheasant
Pickle
Pimento
Pineapple
Pineapple (from a can)
Pineapple juice without sugar
Pinto beans speckled
Pistachios
Plaice
Plum
Plums
Pomegranate
Poppy
Potato flour
Prickly pear
Psyllium seed
Pudding powder vanilla
Pumpernickel (dark bread)
Pumpkin seed oil
Pumpkin seeds
Quinoa
Rabbit
Rabbit (wild)
Radish black
Radish leaves
Raspberry leaf tea
Red berry (without sugar)
Red cabbage
Red wine
Reishi mushroom
Ribworttea
Rice (fragrance)
Rice (Gaoliang / Sorghum)
Rice Basmati
Rice black
Rice flour
Rice long grain rice
Rice malt

Rice mash
Rice noodles
Rice red
Rice round grain
Rice starch
Rice sticky
Rice sweet
Rice variety any
Rice wild (nature rice)
Romaine lettuce / lettuce salad
Rose blossom tea
Rose leaf tea
Rosefish
Rosemary
Rusk
Rye
Rye flour
Rye wholemeal bread
Safflower (Dyer's thistle / Hong Hua)
Saffron
Sago (cereals)
Sauerkraut (cutted cabbage fermented)
Savoy cabbage / kale
Sea buckthorn
Sea cucumber
Sesame, black
Sesame, white
Shark
Sheep's milk
Sheep's milk yoghurt
Skim milk powder
Sorrel
Sour cherries
Sour cream 15% fat
Sourdough
Soy flour
Soy noodles
Soy sauce
Soy Tofu
Soy Tofu smoked
Soya Cuisine (soy cream)
Soybean milk
Soybeans
Soybeans, black
Soybeans, blacks, fermented
Soybeans, yellow
Spelled (Dark) bread
Spelled flakes
Spelled grain
Spelled semolina
Spelled wholemeal flour
Spinach
Spurdog (spiny dogfish, Schillerlocken)
Star anise

Stevia (candyleaf, sweetleaf)
Sunflower seeds
Sweet potato
Tabasco
Tangerine
Tarragon (Estragon)
Tea mixture uric acid lowering
Thyme
Toast bread (whole grain)
Tomato dried
Tonic Water
Topinambur
Trout
Trout (smoked)
Truffle
Tsampa (roasted barley flour)
Umeboshi paste
Umeboshi plums (Japanese apricots)
Valerian
Vanilla
Vanilla pod
Vanilla powder
Vinegar (Red wine vinegar)
Vinegar Aceto Balsamico white

Walnuts
Walnuts roasted
Water
Wheat
Wheat bran
Wheat bulgur
Wheat flakes
Wheat flour whole grain
Wheat semolina
Wheat semolina for children
Wheat/Rye/Gray-black bread with yeast
Wheatgrass juice
Wheatgrass powder
White beans
White cabbage
White wine
Whitefish
Wild strawberries
Wormwood
Wormwood herb
Yam root, yam root tuber
Yeast
Yogi tea

10.3 Use ingredients: little

Almond milk
Almond puree
Apricot dried
Apricot jam
Apricot nectar
Apricots juice
Basic recipe for a beef soup
Basic recipe for a beef soup (warming)
Basic recipe for a chicken soup (warming)
Bean oil
Beef fillet
Beef meat
Beef meat (calf)
Beef meatbones
Beef Oxtail pieces
Beef soup meat
Beer (alcohol-free)
Beer (alcohol-reduced)
Beer (Pils)
Beer (Top-fermented German dark beer)
Blackberry jam
Blueberry jam
Blueberry juice
Bread roll

Breadcrumbs (wheat bread, bread roll)
Brown ale
Cherry juice
Chestnut puree
Chestnuts
Chicken egg
Chicken meat
Chicken yolk
Cola drink (low calorie)
Corn germ oil
Cow's milk (whole milk 3.5% fat)
Cranberry jam
Cream sour 20%
Currant jam (black)
Currant jam (red)
Currant juice (black)
Currants (black)
Currants (red)
Dates dried
Dates red
Deer meat
Deer meat
Deer's Bones
Ducks egg
Edam cheese
Evening primrose oil

Fernet Branca (herbal bitter liqueur)
Feta cheese
Feta cheese
Fig dried
Fish sauce
Fresh cheese
Fresh cheese with herbs
Fructose (glucose)
Fruit mix juice
Ginger oil
Ginseng liqueur
Goat
Goose egg
Gouda cheese
Grape juice red
Grape juice white
Honey
Honey wine (Met)
Horse meat
Ladyfingers
Lamb bones
Lamb meat
Lamb shoulder
Lychee liqueur
Mango juice
Maple syrup
Margarine
Margarine (diet)
Martini
Mold cheese
Mozzarella
Mutton
Noodles (wheat) with egg
Noodles (wheat, lasagne) with egg
Noodles (wheat, ribbon noodles) with egg
Noodles (wheat, spaghetti) with egg
Orange jam
Orange juice
Palm oil
Peanut (roasted)
Peanut oil
Peanuts
Pear juice
Pigeon
Pigeon egg
Plum dried
Pork Bacon
Pork ham
Pork ham cooked
Pork ham smoked
Pork knuckle
Pork meat

Processed cheese 12%
Prosecco
Quail egg
Rabbit meat
Raisins
Raspberry jam
Rum
Sake
Salt
Salt (herbal)
Sesame oil
Sesame oil roasted
Sesame paste (Tahini)
Sherry (whine)
Shiitake, dried
Soybean oil
Spirit
Strawberry jam
Strawberry Juice
Sugar - icing sugar
Sugar brown
Sugar candy white
Sugar cane sugar
Sugar fructose - fruit sugar
Sugar glucose - grapes sugar
Sugar Milk Sugar
Sugar molasses
Sugar palm sugar
Sugar substitute (sweetener)
Sugar white
Sunflower oil
Thistle oil
Turkey breast meat
Turkey ham
Vanilla sugar natural
Wheat beer
Wheat flatbread/pita bread
Wheat flour
White bread (baguette)
White bread (pretzel sticks)
White bread (roll)
White bread (wheat bread)
White breadcrumbs
White dumpling bread (wheat bread cut into chunks)
Wild boar meat
Yoghurt vanilla
Yogurt (natural, 3.5% fat)

10.4 Do not use contra-acting foods

Almond marzipan
Basic recipe for a duck soup
Beef bone marrow
Beef heart
Beef heart (calf)
Beef kidney
Beef liver
Beef lungs (calf)
Beef stomach
Brie cheese
Butter (half fat)
Butter organic
Calamari
Camembert
Campari
Carp
Caviar
Chicken Blood
Chicken heart
Chicken liver
Chicken stomach
Chickweed
Chocolate
Chocolate (Diabetic)
Clarified butter
Coconut fat
Cola drink
Cooking oil
Crab
Cream (30% fat)
Cream sour 30%
Cream, sweet 30%
Créme fraiche cheese
Curd cheese 40%
Deer's kidneys
Duck (heart)
Duck (slaughtered)
Eel
Eel smoked
Emmental cheese
Fish innards
Fish remains
Freshwater crab
Goat and sheep's liver
Goose
Goose blood
Goose fat

Goose parts
Gorgonzola
Grass carp
Greengage
Jellyfish
Lamb kidneys
Lamb liver
Lobster
Longane
Mayonnaise 50%
Mayonnaise 80%
Morel (black, dried)
Morel, dried
Mussels
Octopus
Octopus
Oyster mushroom
Oyster shell powder
Oysters
Parmesan
Peanut butter
Pig blood
Pine nuts
Pork brain
Pork fat (lard)
Pork heart
Pork kidneys
Pork Lard
Pork liver
Pork lung
Pork marrow bones
Pork sausage (Bratwurst)
Pork skin
Pork stomach
Pork/beef sausage (smoked)
Pork's intestine
processed cheese 30%
Puff pastry
Quail
Rabbit liver
Seacrab
Shrimp
Shrimps
Slug
Spiny lobsters
Supplementary nutrition

11 Herbs and their effects

11.1 Basil

It has a beneficial effect on flatulence and nausea, relaxing and soothing. Good to fight emphysema, bronchitis, whooping cough, high blood pressure, headache, mouth odor, warts, hiccup, gout, migraine.

11.2 Nettles

Promotes urination. Tea or juice, cleanses the blood and the kidneys, supports prostate problems, inhibit the formation of inflammation, pain-relieving.

11.3 Dill

The medicinal and spice herb has an antispasmodic effect and stimulates gastric juice production. Good to fight flatulence. Antispasmodic for gastrointestinal discomfort.

11.4 Chervil dried

Forces urination, detoxifying, blood-purifying and blood-pressure-reducing effects.

11.5 Coriander

The essential oils are appetizing, digestive, cramping and soothing in stomach and intestinal disorders.

11.6 Herbs various

Appetizing, lots of trace elements and vitamins

11.7 Cress

Diuretic, supports urination. Good to fight dry mouth, inner agitation, sore throat, diabetes, kidney stones, gastrointestinal complaints, lung problems, menstrual cramps or cancer.

11.8 Chives

Bactericide, prevents cancer, strengthens gastric juice production, promotes digestion and blood circulation, promotes growth, triggers stagnation.

11.9 Lovage

Stimulates digestion, reduces pain. Extracts of the root are used to flush out urinary tract infections and prevent kidney gravel.

11.10   Dandelion (young plants)

Detoxifies, relieves inflammation. Regulates digestion, helps with rheumatism, releases kidney stones, leaves pimples and chronic skin disorders disappear.

11.11   Oregano dried

It has an anti-digestive, calming and nerve-strengthening effect, helps to fight cramping stomach and intestinal disorders. The ingredient Carvacrol has an anti-inflammatory effect.

11.12   Parsley

Stimulates liver function, detoxifies. Forces urinating. Relieves flatulence. Digestive and menstrual stimulating, birth-accelerating, memory-enhancing, blood-purifying, skin-smoothing.

11.13   Peppermint

Relaxes, frees the lungs and the nose (inhale), regulates the cycle. Stimulates bile flow and bile production, antispasmodic in gastrointestinal disorders, antimicrobial and antiviral.

11.14   Rosemary

Promotes digestion, relieves bloating, strengthens lung, spleen and kidney. Affects the circulation and nerves. Appetizing. Baths help to fight circulatory disorders as well as with gout and rheumatism.

11.15   Sage

Good to fight yeast infections. The leaves have a digestive effect and are used in greasy foods. Antiperspirant effect. Helps to relieve coughing attacks. Dries out (TCM).

11.16   Black caraway

Detoxifying, immunoregulatory. In addition, the oil should stimulate the formation of bone marrow cells and generally protect body cells from viruses.

11.17 Thyme dried

Disinfecting. It stimulates the blood circulation, increases the appetite and helps to digest fat meat better. Strengthens lungs and spleen (TCM).

11.18 Lemon Balm (fresh)

Stimulating, antibacterial, encouraging, relaxing, antispasmodic, cooling, antipyretic, analgesic, sweat-inducing, virus-inhibiting. Good for colds, fever, flu, cough, bronchitis, asthma, loss of appetite, bloating, heartburn.

12 Basics of Nutrition

The basic principles of nutrition described herein are general recommendations. They are not aimed at a specific form of therapy. Recommendations concerning a therapy have priority.

12.1 Nutrition

Regular meals in a relaxed atmosphere. A warm breakfast is considered a good start into the day.
The main meals ought to be taken for lunch – supper in the early evening. Pay attention to feeling hungry or sated: don't eat too much nor remain hungry is the rule
Prepare the meals freshly from natural, regional products. Frozen, heat-conserved, industrially prepared or foodstuffs cooked in the microwave oven are rejected.
Choice of foodstuffs according to the season: more cooling food in summer, more warming food in winter.
Eat cooked food at least twice a day. Food and drinks ought to be lukewarm, never ice-cold or hot.
Raw vegetables, briefly cooked vegetables, freshly squeezed juices and mineral water are not recommended. Milk and dairy products are only included in the diet if they don't cause problems.
Don't use therapeutic recipes over a longer period without consulting your doctor or therapist.

Varied food
Enjoy the diversity of foodstuffs. Characteristics of a balanced nutrition are variety, suitable combination and a balanced quantity of rich and low energy foodstuffs (on one hand avoiding undersupply with essential nutrients and on the other hand to take to many undesirable substances).

A lot of Cereal Products - and Potatoes
Bread, pasta, rice, cereal flakes (best wholemeal) as well as potatoes contain almost no fat, but many vitamins, mineral nutrients, trace elements, roughage and secondary plant substances. These foodstuffs ought to be taken with low-fat side dishes.

Vegetables and Fruit – „Take Five" every day ...
5 portions of vegetables and fruit a day, as fresh as possible, briefly cooked, or maybe one portion as a juice – ideal as a side dish to every meal as well as snack between meals: Thus a lot of vitamins, mineral nutrients as well as roughage and secondary plant substances

Daily milk and dairy products
Milk and Dairy Products every Day, once or twice per Week Fish;
meat, sausages as well as eggs moderately. These foodstuffs contain
valuable nutrients like calcium in the milk, iodine selenium and omega-3
fat acids in saltwater fish. Meat is favorable due to its high content of
disposable iron and the vitamins B1, B6 and B12. Quantities of 300 – 600
g meat and sausage per week are sufficient. Prefer low-fat products,
especially in meat- and dairy products.

Low-fat and fatty Foodstuffs
Fat supplies us with essential fat acids and fatty foodstuffs contain also
fat-soluble vitamins. Fat is high in energy; therefore much fat in the food
may cause overweight, possibly also cancer. Too many saturated fat
acids may further a tendency for cardio-vascular diseases in the long
term. Prefer vegetable oils and fats (e.g. rapeseed-, olive-, soya-oils and
solid fats produced therefrom). Beware of invisible fat in meat- and dairy
products, pastry and sweets as well as in fast-food and convenience
foods. 70 – 90 g fat per day is sufficient.

Moderately Sugar and Salt
Take sugar and foods/drinks containing various kinds of sugar (e.g.
glucose syrup) only occasionally. Use herbs and spices as well as a little
salt creatively. Prefer salt containing iodine.

Plenty of Liquids
Water is absolutely essential. Drink 1-2 l liquids every day. Prefer water
(with or without gas) and other low-calorie drinks. Alcoholic drinks should
not be taken.

Tasty Dishes, carefully cooked
Cook the meals with as low temperatures and as short as possible, using
little water and fat – this preserves the original taste, keeps the nutrients
intact and prevents the production of harmful compounds.

Take time and enjoy the food
Take your Time and enjoy your Food
Eating consciously helps to eat right. The eye enjoys food, too. It's fun,
invites to enjoy varied dishes and stimulates the feeling of satiety.

Watch your Weight and stay in Motion
A balanced diet and a lot of exercise and sport (30 – 60 min/day) are a
healthy combination. The right weight furthers well-being and health.
Thermals, directional effectiveness, digestive power

There are various criteria for judging the effectiveness of herbs and foodstuffs.
The use of certain herbs and ingredients is based on observations of the effects on the body which these foodstuffs, herbs and spices show after having eaten them. The medical science has developed following system: Every ingredient or herb has a directional effectiveness. Furthermore, there are herbs which have a special effect on certain organs.
The basic condition for a healthy metabolism is to obtain sufficient energy from food and that the digestive process doesn't use too much energy. An easily digestible meal makes content and sated, doesn't cause flatulence and fatigue after the meal. The perfect spices increase the healthiness of our meals. Very often, just small doses of herbs and spices will suffice. They are not used to make us sated, but to help our digestive organs to digest the food.

12.2 Recipes

The recipes list the ingredients to be used and the cooking instructions show how the dish is prepared. The list of ingredients shows the concerned quantities as well as the relevance for the therapy. If you find „less than mentioned", try to comply or find an alternative from the „list of recommended foodstuffs". Mostly it shall result just in a small change of taste when you simply avoid this ingredient.
Mild cooking methods: boiling, stewing, poaching, steaming
Strong cooking methods: barbecuing, roasting, frying, smoking
Balanced cooking methods: deep-frying, baking brick
Deep-freezing and warming in the microwave oven should be avoided (denaturalization).

12.3 Foodstuffs

Foodstuffs have an effect on body and soul like medicinal herbs, only a very much milder one. Dietary advice is mainly based on regional foodstuffs. The knowledge about the effects of each foodstuff and the knowledge, when which foodstuff shall be used, is based on the orthodoschool of medicine. Use ecologic-organic products, if possible. As everything should be cooked for a long time due to a better digestability and very rarely eaten raw, the food agrees with everyone.
The classification of the foodstuffs according to their effect on the body is the basis in order to achieve a harmonious status of health.

Dietary advisors do not recommend certain foodstuffs for everyone. The individual diet is tailor-made for the individual constitution.

Buy only fresh and ripe fruit and vegetables. You ought to leave unripe fruit and vegetables and such with brown spots and wilted leaves behind in the market. In this case take deep-frozen goods (never ready-to-serve dishes!). Fruit and vegetables are deep-frozen immediately after harvesting and often contain more vitamins and minerals than the goods from the vegetable shelf. Whereas conserved or tinned goods contain very much less biological substances. Also, salt, sugar and others are mostly added to the latter. Never leave the foodstuffs in the water after washing them to avoid that many vital substances get drowned. Clean salads, fruit and vegetables immediately before serving.

Please make sure of the hygienic processing of foodstuffs. Clean your salads, fruit and vegetables carefully. When cooking with meat, prepare all ingredients first and then process the meat products. Clean the worktop and tools very carefully. Wooden surfaces ought to be treated with a mild disinfectant regularly in order to reduce germination.

Store fruit and vegetables separately, if possible. Harvested fruit and vegetables are still alive and emit e.g. ethylene gas, which makes other products ripen and age faster. Keep meat and fish in the closed packaging or store them in the fridge in closed containers.

12.4 Herbs

There are some basic rules for storing medicinal herbs. On principle, herbs must be protected from direct sunlight, humidity and heat.

Containers for the storage of herbs may be glasses, ceramic jars and even plastic containers. However, plastic is a rather unsuitable material and should only be a short-term solution. In case of glass containers, use a dark material.

Medicinal herbs cannot be kept for any long period. The shelf life of herbs is limited. However, it can be prolonged with suitable storage. The place should be dark, rather cool and absolutely dry. A wooden medicine cabinet, placed not directly next to a source of heat, would be ideal. Never buy large quantities of herbs so as not to have to throw them away. Label the container with the name of the herb and the date of harvesting or processing.

13 Other dietic-books

The following syndromes of dietetics, TCM or for a therapy supplement for cancer are available.

Dietetics

E001. Nutrition of the infant - baby food
E002. Nutrition during lactation
E003. Nutrition in old age
E004. Nutrition of children and adolescents
E005. Nutrition of athletes
E006. Light weight
E007. Pregnancy
E008. Full food

Protein and electrolyte - kidneys
E009. (hemodialysis) dialysis treatment
E010. Acute renal failure
E011. Chronic renal insufficiency
E012. Nephrotic syndrome
E013. Kidney stones (nephrolithiasis)

Gastrointestinal tract - pancreas
E014. Acute pancreatitis (inflammation of the pancreas)
E015. Chronic pancreatitis (inflammation of the pancreas)

Gastrointestinal tract - small intestine and large intestine
E016. Acute obstipation (constipation)
E017. Chronic obstipation (constipation)
E018. Colon irritabile
E019. Diverticulitis
E020. Acquired lactose intolerance (lactose malabsorption)
E021. Fructose malabsorption
E022. Glutensensitive enteropathy (celiac disease)
E023. Colectomy
E024. Short Bowel Syndrome

Gastrointestinal tract - liver, gallbladder, bile ducts
E025. Acute and chronic hepatitis (inflammation of the liver)
E026. Cholelithiasis (bile stones)
E027. fatty liver
E028. cirrhosis

Gastrointestinal tract - Stomach and duodenal intestine
E029. Acute gastritis
E030. Chronic gastritis
E031. Stomach bleeding
E032. Ulcus ventriculi and duodenal ulcer
E033. Condition after gastric surgery

Gastrointestinal tract - oral cavity and esophagus
E034. Stomatitis
E035. Esophageal carcinoma (esophageal cancer)
E036. Refluosophagitis (heartburn)

Special diseases
E037. Phenylketonuria (PKU)
E038. Rheumatic joint diseases

Metabolism
E039. Obesity (overweight)
E040. Diabetes mellitus
E041. Eating disorders (underweight)

Fat metabolism
E042. Hypercholesterolaemia (increased cholesterol level)
E043. Hepatic Encephalopathy

Heart and circulation
E044. Arteriosclerosis (arterial calcification)
E045. Heart insufficiency
E046. Hypertension
E047. Hyperuricaemia and gout

Changed nutrient requirements
E048. In case of fever
E049. For malignant diseases
E050. After burns
E051. Radiation and chemotherapy

CANCER
E100. Pancreatic cancer
E101. Bladder cancer
E102. Blood cancer (leukemia)
E103. Breast cancer
E104. Colorectal cancer
E105. Gastric cancer
E106. Kidney cancer
E107. Esophageal cancer

TCM
E200. Bladder - moisture heat in the bladder
E201. Bladder - moisture and cold in the bladder
E202. Bladder - emptiness and cold in the bladder
E203. Large intestine - external cold affects the large intestine
E204. Large intestine - moisture heat in the large intestine
E205. Large intestine - heat blocks the intestine II acute
E206. Large intestine - dryness of the colon
E207. Large intestine - Yang deficiency (cold)
E208. Heart - Blood insufficiency
E209. Heart - Blood stagnation
E210. Heart - Fire
E211. Heart - Hot mucus clogs the heart pores

E212. Heart - Cold mucus clogs the heart pores
E213. Heart - Qi deficiency
E214. Heart - Yang deficiency
E215. Heart - Yin deficiency
E216. Liver - Ascending Liver Yang
E217. Liver - Blood deficiency
E218. Liver - Blood stagnation
E219. Liver - Moisture heat in liver and gall bladder
E220. Liver - Fire
E221. Liver - Gall bladder Qi-Empty
E222. Liver - Cold in the liver meridian
E223. Liver - Qi stagnation
E224. Liver - Wind
E225. Liver - Wind with ascending liver Yang
E226. Liver - Wind with blood anemic
E227. Liver - Wind with extreme heat
E228. Lung - Qi deficiency
E229. Lung - Mucus-moisture in the lungs
E230. Lung - Mucus-heat in the lungs
E231. Lung - Mucus-cold in the lungs
E232. Lung - Dryness of the lungs
E233. Lung - Wind-heat attacks the lungs
E234. Lung - Wind-cold affects the lungs
E235. Lung - Yin deficiency
E236. Stomach - Bloodstagnation
E237. Stomach - Fire
E238. Stomach - Cold with liquid
E239. Stomach - Nutrition stagnation
E240. Stomach - Qi deficiency
E241. Stomach - Rebellious Qi
E242. Stomach - Yin Emptiness
E243. Spleen - Heat and moisture attack the spleen
E244. Spleen - Coldness and moisture affects the spleen
E245. Spleen - Qi deficiency
E246. Spleen - Qi deficiency + Declining spleen Qi
E247. Spleen - Qi deficiency + spleen does not control the blood
E248. Spleen - Yang deficiency
E249. Kidney - Heart and kidney no longer communicate
E250. Kidney - Jing deficiency
E251. Kidney - Kidneys cannot receive the Qi
E252. Kidney - Qi is not stable
E253. Kidney - Yang deficiency
E254. Kidney - Yin deficiency

For further information visit di-book.com.